Competence-based Teaching and Training

City & Guilds Co-publishing Series

City & Guilds has a long history of providing assessments and certification to those who have undertaken education and training in a wide variety of technical subjects or occupational areas. Its business is essentially to provide an assurance that pre-determined standards have been met. That activity has grown in importance over the past few years as government and national bodies strive to create the right conditions for the steady growth of a skilled and flexible workforce.

Both teachers and learners need materials to support them as they work towards the attainment of qualifications, and City & Guilds is pleased to be working with several distinguished publishers towards meeting that need. It has been closely involved in planning, author selection and text appraisal, although the opinions expressed in the publications are those of the individual authors.

Competence-based Teaching and Training

Anne Castling

City&
Guilds

THOMSON

LEARNING

Australia · Canada · Mexico · Singapore · Spain · United Kingdom · United States

Competence-based Teaching and Training

The Thomson Learning logo is a registered trademark used herein under licence.

For more information, contact Thomson Learning, Berkshire House, 168–173 High Holborn, London, WC1V 7AA or visit us on the World Wide Web at:
http://www.thomsonlearning.co.uk

British Library Cataloguing-in-Publication Data
A catalogue record for this book is available from the British Library

ISBN 1-86152-737-3

First published by MacMillan Press 1996
Reprinted 2001 by Thomson Learning

Printed by TJ International Ltd., Padstow, Cornwall

FOR DAVID, FREDA AND SYDNEY

Acknowledgements

I would like to thank the following people for their support and guidance during the writing of this book:

John Berry-Richards, Lewis Jones and Andrew Reeves for their feedback on each chapter as it was produced, and for their insights, constructive criticism and positive suggestions at every stage;

David Sims for his unfailing interest, continuous encouragement and helpful comments on the language used;

My own students in the north-east and south-east of England who feature in these pages and are the best of the book;

My colleagues, both tutors and verifiers, who have shared their wisdom and enthusiasm over the years;

Anne Webster at Macmillan for sensitive and supportive guidance.

The author and publishers wish to thank the following for permission to use copyright material:

Andrew Reeves for the diagrams on pages 2 and 142;

Faber and Faber Limited for the quotation from *The Four Quartets* by T.S. Eliot on page 1.

Contents

Preface

This book is intended as a guide for anyone who is seeking to develop their teaching or training skills, whether they are learning on a course or studying independently.

It will be found helpful by all those who are supporting the learning of adults, whether their context is further and adult education, business or professional training or youth and community work.

The book is designed as an essential text for those following a systematic programme of teacher training, such as the City & Guilds Further and Adult Education Teachers' Certificate (7306 and 7307), the RSA Examinations Board suite of teacher training programmes and the first year of many Certificate in Education (FE) programmes. It will also be useful to candidates working towards the NVQ/SVQ level 3 or level 4 in Training and Development.

The content of the book follows closely the material of the Training and Development NVQs/SVQs at levels 3 and 4. All the performance criteria are covered, including the knowledge and understanding, skills, attitudes and values. An Appendix shows the exact match between the chapters and the relevant units and elements. Within the text itself, I have used straightforward language.

The book is organised to follow the stages of the teaching and training cycle from the identification of learning needs through planning and delivery to assessment and evaluation. The chapters follow this sequence but each can also be read independently.

A particular feature of the book is the use throughout the chapters of case studies and examples drawn from real teaching and training situations with which the reader can identify immediately.

This book does not aim to replace established or more detailed texts on teacher education and training, such as the companion text by David Minton, *Teaching Skills in Further and Adult Education*. At the end of the book readers will find Suggestions for Further Reading which will help them to extend their understanding of the material presented here.

The terms **teacher** and **trainer** are used interchangeably, as are the terms **learner**, **student** and **trainee**, to indicate that we are all engaged in a shared enterprise, whatever our particular context and preferred terminology.

ANNE CASTLING

1 Introduction

In my end is my beginning.

T. S. Eliot, 'East Coker' in *The Four Quartets*

This book introduces you to the knowledge, understanding, skills, attitudes and values you need to develop, to become an effective teacher or trainer of both younger and older adults. These attributes, taken together, add up to your competence and your professionalism.

In the context of this book, the concept of teaching competence implies a very high standard. It includes complex skills such as planning, organising yourself and others, communicating effectively in a range of contexts and evaluating your own practice. It calls for attitudes such as flexibility and openness to learning with and from other people. It asks you to develop such values as respect for the individuality of each learner.

The nature of teaching

Teaching is in equal parts an art, a science and a craft. It is an integrated process rather than a series of unrelated activities. At its heart is the learner, not the teacher. All the varied activities which you undertake have the same aim, that of promoting learning.

As you work through this book you will see that these rather grand concepts can be translated into everyday activities which will help to bring about successful learning. For although teaching is an holistic activity, it helps enormously when you are learning its mysteries to be able to break it down into smaller processes. It is also useful to refer to a model or framework which shows how the pieces of the overall design fit together.

The teaching/training cycle

Crucial to the organisation of this book is the concept of a teaching or training cycle. Figure 1.1 shows a model which will help you to relate the parts.

This is a cycle of interlinked processes. Each stage leads logically to the next. Your work in analysing students' learning needs leads you naturally to plan learning routes for them to follow. Your planning leads to programmes variously delivered, during and after which you monitor students' learning and assess their achievements. You

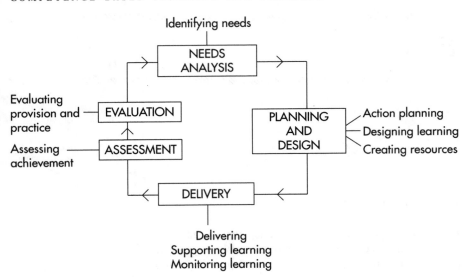

Identifying needs

NEEDS ANALYSIS

Evaluating provision and practice — EVALUATION

Assessing achievement — ASSESSMENT

PLANNING AND DESIGN

Action planning
Designing learning
Creating resources

DELIVERY

Delivering
Supporting learning
Monitoring learning

◀ **Figure 1.1**
The teaching/training cycle (courtesy of Andrew Reeves).

then evaluate **your** effectiveness at each stage of the cycle. This review leads you to adapt your practice, beginning with your investigation of learners' needs, and off you go round the cycle again.

There are also links across the cycle. The objectives you set at the planning stage provide the basis for your assessment scheme. The learning needs which you helped learners identify initially become the basis of your review of their progress.

The chapters of the book follow this cycle. You may prefer to read them in this order, or you could start at a point of particular interest to you and then follow your own logic. For example, you could begin by looking at the teaching of skills; this could lead you on from coaching to supporting individual learners or to teaching aids and learning resources.

Assumptions about teaching and learning

These assumptions run throughout the book. They are:

- that a systematic approach to teaching is beneficial to your learners, your colleagues and yourself;
- that learning is a deeply personal, individual process for each of us;
- that you teach people first, and subject material second;
- that learning is a richer and more rewarding process if it can be shared with other people;
- that risks are worth taking and mistakes can be growth points;
- that experience only leads to change if it is filtered through reflection;
- that development takes courage as well as imagination;
- that the most useful attribute you can develop as a teacher or trainer is flexibility.

This book is full of small case studies and examples of teachers planning their actions, taking risks, using their imagination to respond to students' needs, consulting each other, and adapting their practice as circumstances or demands change. You could not have a better model for your own exploration of your role, responsibilities and skills.

You will also find many suggested activities in the text. These will prompt you to make decisions of your own before moving on to look at the solutions offered.

You might now like to refresh your grasp of the way competence-based learning works by reading through the next section of this introduction.

The development of competence-based qualifications

You are probably aware of the developments in the provision of national vocational qualifications which have been taking place for a number of years. The National Council for Vocational Qualifications (NCVQ) has been working with representative groups of employers, called Lead Bodies or Occupational Standards Councils, and organisations which award qualifications, such as City & Guilds, to redesign existing qualifications and develop new ones.

NCVQ had two key aims: to rationalise the often confusing and very wide range of existing qualifications, and to bring them into line with employers' requirements for competence in the workplace. Where qualifications existed, it was sometimes difficult to see if or how one equated to another, or how the more theoretical aspects of a qualification related to the practical nature of the job itself.

Some occupational areas lacked qualifications at appropriate levels for the staff employed, so that even if employees were demonstrating their competence at work, there was no way of accrediting this.

The Government was also concerned that many people who began to work towards qualifications failed to complete them and so were left with no evidence of achievement.

Key concepts underlying National and Scottish Vocational Qualifications

Certain principles guided the development of NVQs/SVQs:

- achievement should be based on the concept of **competence**, or demonstrated ability to perform to given standards;
- competence should be defined largely in terms of performance **in the workplace** and employers should define the **standards** to be met;
- **access** to these vocational qualifications should be as wide as possible – they should not depend on having to attend courses of study at set times in set places for set periods, although they could continue to be gained in this way;
- assessment, therefore, could be carried out in the workplace **by suitably trained and qualified workplace assessors**;
- occupational competence would be defined at different **levels**; there would be a narrow band of levels (1–5) representing increasing degrees of responsibility and autonomy in the workplace (not higher academic attainment);
- since competence was, by definition, achievement of all the skills and knowledge required, a **pass/not yet competent** grade was all that could be given;

- progression would depend on gaining more units of competence at the same level or attaining a higher level **as job responsibilities increased**;
- although there was a broad equivalence between the levels of vocational and academic qualifications, the routes were parallel rather than interlocking;
- all candidates for qualifications should have **access to fair and reliable assessment** – therefore, all candidates should have an equal opportunity to succeed, standards should be written to facilitate unambiguous interpretation, **all assessors should be trained and qualified** and all assessment should be subject to rigorous quality assurance procedures (**internal and external verification**);
- candidates could demonstrate their competence in several ways, including through **the accreditation of their prior learning** – they could be considered competent if they could present sufficient valid and reliable evidence of current competence in an appropriate range of contexts, without having to undertake any further training or experience.

Characteristics of NVQs

You can see that certain features of the qualifications follow from these design principles. In order, for instance, for assessment to be fair and reliable, the standards of competence must be explicit. They must be detailed and specific, so that all assessors interpret them in the same way. This leads to a description of workplace performance by means of a series of performance criteria. The candidates use the criteria to build up an accurate model of what is required, so that they are able to prepare themselves satisfactorily for assessment.

So that an assessor can feel confident in the candidates' performance, they may have to demonstrate it several times and in a range of contexts; for instance, serving food in a silver service restaurant, a service restaurant, and a fast food outlet. Similarly, they will have to show that they **understand** their own actions and are not just performing in robotic fashion. They will also be questioned, either orally or in writing.

In order to deal with the problem of unfinished business, of students falling out before completing their qualifications, the occupational area is broken up into a series of areas of activity. These are then designated **units of competence**, and candidates can gain accreditation for as many of these as they can manage. At a later date they can attain any remaining units to complete their full qualification. The units themselves are divided into **elements of competence**, which represent subsections of the activity described in the larger unit.

Because candidates are **proving** their competence, the proof is called **evidence**. It is organised into a file which is called a **portfolio**. Evidence can take more varied forms than traditional examinations or coursework sometimes allow. It can include statements from suitably placed and qualified people who witness the candidates' competence, for example, a colleague in the workplace or a teacher/trainer on a course taken earlier. It can include video and audio tapes, photographs, reports on practical performance, records of oral questioning and task-based assignments.

In order to guarantee that assessments would be fair and reliable, NCVQ felt that it had to set up a **quality assurance** system of checks at several stages. All assessors of NVQ programmes have to achieve a qualification such as the City & Guilds **Vocational Assessor's Award** to show that they are competent to carry out direct assessment or to assess candidates using evidence from several sources. They must achieve two Training and Development units: D32 (Assess candidate performance) and D33 (Assess candidate using differing sources of evidence). You may well have these, or be working towards them.

At the next stage, each assessor has a sample of their work checked by a colleague in their place of work, called an **internal verifier**. This person is checked on in turn by a representative of the relevant awarding body, who is called an **external verifier**. Both internal and external verifiers check assessment procedures and practice in order to confirm that what should be happening, is happening, and that what should have happened, has happened. Internal verifiers work to a policy set up in their workplace, derived from their awarding body's guidelines which, in turn, echo NCVQ policy. External verifiers are regulated by their awarding body which is, again, following NCVQ policy.

Characteristics of GNVQs

You may be familiar with the parallel development of General National Vocational Qualifications (GNVQs). These are alternatives to A levels or to GCSEs which develop the knowledge, understanding and skills needed for broad areas of work. They were developed mainly for young people in full-time education but have since become available as part-time courses and for adults. They follow some of the design principles of NVQs, such as the division into units and elements of competence, but with some important differences. These differences include:

- they are related in a general way to occupational areas but they are not specifically about particular occupations;
- they include core skills of communication, application of number and use of computers;
- they are offered at three levels, Foundation, Intermediate and Advanced;
- they are tested by means of coursework and external exams;
- results are graded pass, merit and distinction.

If you assess on a GNVQ programme, you, too, will need to qualify as an assessor, and have your work checked by an internal and external verifier.

Getting involved in competence-based teaching and training

You may already be working on NVQ or GNVQ programmes, in which case you will appreciate the significance of the changes described above. Even if you are not involved as yet, you need to know about these changes, because they are the main focus of current developments in further education and training. It is helpful to understand how the system overall is changing and how it is affecting many colleagues, students and trainees.

The development of competence-based qualifications is a controversial issue, causing much debate at all levels within teaching and training. As a member of the profession you need to understand how the competence-based system works, in order to be part of the debate, to discuss its advantages and disadvantages, and to evaluate the contribution of NVQs and GNVQs to the education and training of adults and young people.

In the chapters which follow you will find frequent references to the competence-based approach to teaching and training. However, it is not necessary to be working within this system to gain value from the text. The principles and strategies discussed apply equally well to competence or other more established forms of teaching and training.

Why not move on now to the next chapter *Getting Started?*

2 Getting Started

Let's begin by looking at ways in which teachers and trainers can make learners feel that they are in the right place, with the right people, and doing the right things to help them reach their particular learning goals.

This chapter is all about helping learners feel 'at home', in the sense that they feel from their first contact with you that they are known, are important and will be helped to succeed. This requires certain things of you, their teacher or trainer.

First of all you will need to know about the learning opportunities which are offered either in your workplace or locally, so that you can advise and guide learners from the outset. Then you will need to devise ways of finding out about your learners and their needs so that you can help them match their goals to the learning opportunities which you can offer.

This is not just a mechanical process. You will be looking in this chapter at ways of creating good working relationships with students and trainees at every stage of their learning, from initial guidance onwards. This means thinking about the many ways in which learners differ in their needs and ways of learning, and how you can help to provide each of them with equal opportunities to learn and to achieve.

You are going to look at strategies you can adopt to create these opportunities and to prevent discrimination occurring. You will need to think about the needs of all your learners, particularly those who have learning difficulties or disabilities.

Getting it right – your part in the process

Creating the right kind of learning environment means much more than having a pleasant reception area and glossy leaflets. It involves everyone with responsibility for any part of the learning process, but it is the individual teacher or trainer who has most influence and effect on learners. Potential students need to feel that the people and the place are right for them – for their age group, for their gender, for their physical and personal needs as well as for their learning needs. Actual students need to feel known, understood, guided, supported and fairly treated by their teachers and assessors. They need to feel that you are 'on their side'.

This requires careful planning and lots of attention to detail by both organisations as a whole and individual staff, whether in a college, training centre, assessment centre or within any workplace where learning and assessment are set up.

Where do you come in?

Imagine that you are going to have responsibility for a group of learners in your own subject or skill area for several weeks. What can **you** do at the various stages of their learning programme to make sure that they get a good deal?

Make a list of about a dozen points, then look at the suggestions which follow. You could:

- get to know the organisation(s) where you teach or train – the purpose, structure, style, key people as well as the learning programmes on offer;
- get to know your learners' background, goals and abilities;
- think out your own code of behaviour, the way you work with colleagues, individual students and groups;
- negotiate for rooms and facilities appropriate to your learners' needs and objectives, including physical access and comfort – make sure they meet Health and Safety criteria;
- plan teaching/training and assessment activities to suit your learners' needs and circumstances;
- produce learning and assessment materials which are motivating and do not put anyone at a disadvantage;
- use teaching and assessment approaches which suit this particular group;
- negotiate guidelines for all group members to follow so that no one is treated unfairly;
- find out about all the sources of help your group can use and tell them how to do so;
- give them tutorial support – use it to build confidence and show them their progress;
- carry out fair and reliable assessment;
- deal with any instances of discrimination if they arise in the course of the group's learning and assessment;
- consult the group about your management of their learning programme – use their views to make changes if needed.

You can see that if you follow this kind of sequence, you will be playing your part in creating the right kind of climate for learning at each stage of the teaching/training cycle which we looked at in the introductory chapter.

Identifying the opportunities on offer

An important step in creating the right kind of learning environment for students is to identify what their needs and preferences are – not just for qualifications but also for the ways in which they would prefer to study, and the styles of teaching or training which they would like to experience. However, to make a match between these preferences and what you can offer, you need to know what is available. You may

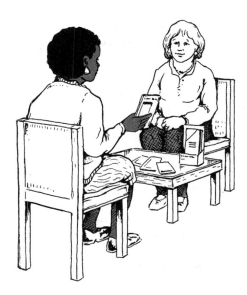

◀ **Figure 2.1**
Helping students and
learners make their
choices.

need to do some research. You can be most helpful to enquirers if you know about wider opportunities within your vocational area and about other provisions in the locality, if you are unable to offer what is needed in your own place of work.

You will also need to know about the support facilities and services your organisation can offer for those with physical, financial or family needs which must be catered for before they are able to study. Find out about language support for students whose first language is not English, disability support for a student using a wheelchair, information technology (IT) support, crèche facilities, and so on.

When you have completed your research you will be able to give advice either to people enquiring about learning opportunities, or to your own student group whom you identified in the previous activity, at any stage of their learning.

Identifying what you need to know

Think about the kind of information **you** would need to know if you were investigating a possible learning route. It falls into four general categories:

(1) *Different ways in which you can learn*
These could include short or long courses or single training sessions, attendance at a drop-in workshop or open learning centre, individual tutoring or coaching, shadowing an expert worker or doing a work placement.

(2) *Different ways in which your learning can be assessed*
These could include traditional external examinations, continuous assessment of written or practical assignments, accreditation of your prior learning (APL), accreditation for whole qualifications or for units of them, or collecting a portfolio of evidence of your written, oral and practical performance on a number of tasks.

(3) *The kinds of support you can have*

You will remember from earlier in the chapter that support could include study help, for instance with English or IT, numeracy or literacy, as well as financial, careers or personal guidance.

(4) *Practical matters*

This might include information on fees and other costs, entry requirements, equipment or books needed, study facilities, parking, library opening hours, size of learning groups, and so on.

Finding the information you need

You could start in the same place as any other person enquiring about learning opportunities at your place of work. This might be an admissions unit where advisors help people coming in or telephoning for information. It might be a library desk or the reception area of the training section. You could look at the documents which are produced for potential students – the prospectus, guidance leaflets or open day publicity.

You could also talk to a range of people, such as programme managers, course leaders, student advisors, the tutor librarian, an internal verifier, the external verifier, a representative of the awarding bodies, the training manager, or other teachers and trainers. It will be worth keeping a file of the information you discover, and updating it regularly.

The key to successful learning for the **learner** is finding provision which matches their needs, provision which will be both effective and enjoyable. For many adults, the range of possibilities in modern learning organisations will come as a surprise. They will need you to help them evaluate their best route; your role is an important one, because you can inspire and motivate them at this stage as well as give information.

Getting to know your learners' needs

You may be surprised to learn that for many people the motivation to learn is social rather than academic or professional. Their choices are as likely to depend on what their friends are doing as on a work goal. Some may turn down the chance of accreditation of their prior learning (APL) because they would rather join a learning group, despite having done part of the work already. Others will be constrained by home or work circumstances from choosing the options which seem most obvious to you. Yet others will be carrying all sorts of feelings about previous kinds of learning which they have encountered, and this will colour their view of what they want now. Don't expect everyone's choice to be logical or the one which you advise – remember that it is they who will be doing the learning, not you.

What is it that you need to know about your students or trainees before you can get them started on their learning? Situations will vary in detail, but in general a checklist like the one which follows would help you structure an interview, face to face or over the telephone.

You will need to know about each person:

- their learning goals;
- their current abilities;

- their previous achievements;
- their particular needs (gaps in learning, difficulties, disabilities);
- their relevant personal circumstances, such as work schedule and time available for study;
- how they like to learn, such as in a group or one to one;
- how they feel about themselves as learners (degree of confidence, expectations of themselves);
- how they go about studying;
- what they expect from you.

Now you have to decide how you are going to gather this information about your own particular learners, the ones you identified earlier. This will depend on your situation; you may be able to interview or talk to people before they begin their studies, or you may meet them for the first time when they arrive for the first meeting. In either case, remember that this is an opportunity to begin the positive relationship which will help to provide the right climate for their learning. If you are interviewing them, try not to let all the paperwork get in the way, read the application form, the *curriculum vitae* (CV), references and testimonials beforehand if possible, so you can use this valuable time for talking and listening.

Identifying needs after enrolment

There are lots of ways you can find out about your students' needs.

ACTIVITY

See how many tactics you can come up with to find out your students' needs. Then look at the suggestions which follow. You could:

- start with an induction period given over to explaining the type of work and assessment expected of your students, and listen to their queries and comments;
- set a practical test, go round observing each one, talk to them about how they are finding it and begin to plan how you will need to help them;
- meet them individually for a short time before or after the session;
- chat to them informally during coffee time or before the formal session gets under way, but remember to make a note of what you learn;
- telephone them, with their agreement, for a short chat after the first session so that they can share any hopes and fears;
- invite each one to give a 5-minute talk to the group about their goals and expectations;
- give them a questionnaire about their preferences for ways of learning and the help they think they are going to need;
- give them a self-checklist before a new block of material so that you can see the spread of strengths and difficulties. Figure 2.2 shows an example for an NVQ level 2 group in Food Preparation and Cooking.

Food Preparation Skills – my current abilities			
I can	*Not at all*	*Quite well*	*Very well*
Cook with gas			
Cook with electricity			
Use a microwave oven			
Use a food processor			
Use a steamer			
Use a deep fat fryer			
Use metric measurement			
Use imperial measurement			
Chop onions			
Peel potatoes			
Dice carrots			
String celery			
Peel mushrooms			
Skin tomatoes			
De-seed green peppers			

◄ **Figure 2.2**
A useful checklist of skills.

Creating good working relationships with learners

Learning is largely something we do with others and it works much better if there is a positive relationship between teachers and learners, and within learning groups. Many teachers talk about 'creating rapport with learners', by which they mean getting a good learning atmosphere going.

This is not something which only experienced teachers can do. Rapport is the sum of many small but significant activities which you can carry out irrespective of subject area, length of service or type of personality. Some of these activities depend on verbal and non-verbal communication skills, others on organisation and thorough preparation. Rapport is not something applied in the initial encounter and disregarded thereafter, nor does it happen only in group sessions. You will be involved in creating and maintaining good working relationships whenever you meet your students, assess their work or speak to them on the telephone.

ACTIVITY

Imagine two situations for which you are responsible. The first is an interview or tutorial with a learner whom you are meeting for the first time, while the second is a session with a group you teach regularly. How will you set up a positive working relationship in each case?

Initial meetings, particularly with individuals

You could:

- arrange the room and seating so it feels friendly;
- make special arrangements for anyone with particular needs, such as a quiet place and no interruptions for someone with hearing difficulties;

- use the person's name and make sure they know your name;
- look relaxed, make lots of eye contact, and smile;
- invite questions and create opportunities for them;
- listen carefully, and use the information in your exchanges;
- keep to any pre-set time arrangements;
- go at a steady pace and end the meeting calmly;
- make notes immediately afterwards; check these before you meet again so that your student feels properly attended to.

Sessions with groups

You could:

- arrange the seating to encourage interaction between all members of the group, for example, in a U-shape (Figure 2.3);
- sit in the body of the group rather than standing behind a desk;
- arrive early and greet people as they arrive;
- chat in friendly fashion while waiting for stragglers;
- use an ice breaker exercise to help members relate to each other;
- use everyone's name positively during the session;
- have at least one positive interaction with each person;
- make lots of eye contact, smile and use positive gestures;
- share, and if applicable agree, the learning objectives with the students;
- invite points and examples from the group, consult their experience of life and work as well as your own;
- write their ideas on the board or flip chart to show that you value them;
- set an exercise which enables you to circulate and have a quiet word with every-one;
- use visual materials which reflect their world – gender, age, culture, work, leisure.

Now let's look more closely at how you can help to give each learner an equal opportunity to learn and achieve their goals.

◄ Figure 2.3
This kind of layout improves communication.

Working for equality of opportunity

For many potential learners it is not as simple as coming to an organisation for advice, being guided towards a choice of learning route and signing on. There are often barriers to be overcome for students of all ages; many adults juggle work, family and financial responsibilities with the demands of study, while young people may have home and money pressures.

The introduction of national vocational qualifications speeded up a process already underway in many teaching and training establishments, that of opening up access to learning and qualifications to as many people as possible. This means more than structuring the qualification so that credit can be given for each of the parts as well as the whole. You can go on to look at a wide range of strategies in a moment, but first let's examine some of the barriers which some people face when they embark on learning.

ACTIVITY

Here are four small case studies. Brainstorm the difficulties which Maria, Aziz, Zara and Sandro might face, and begin to think of ways in which you might help them to overcome them.

Spot the barriers

Maria is a 40-year-old housewife with three children who wants to pick up a career as a secretary which she gave up 15 years ago to bring up her family. What are the barriers she might have to overcome?

Aziz is a 27-year-old refugee from East Africa recently arrived in England. He has a degree in history but now wants to study accountancy in higher education. What difficulties might he encounter?

Zara is 17 with three brothers between the ages of 4 and 10; her father died last year and her mother is struggling to bring up the children. Zara would like to take a GNVQ course in Leisure and Tourism and hopes to work abroad in the future. What barriers might stand in her way?

Sandro is a security guard for a large business with branches all over the country; the firm is not doing particularly well. He wants to get some qualifications so that he can try for a better job. He respects education but has had very little of it in his 44 years. He wants to join evening classes in Maths and English. What difficulties might he have to cope with?

You probably thought of difficulties to do with money, time for study, a place to study, the need to get to grips with new technology, gender, culture, age, conflicting loyalties and many more. You will not be able to solve every problem but you will be able to make a considerable difference in your role as a teacher or trainer. The more sensitive you are to potential difficulties and the more knowledgeable you are about possible solutions, the more difference you can make for your students. Your attitude alone could be a great support.

Knowing where you stand

Before you begin taking initiatives in support of people whom you feel may be experiencing difficulties or discrimination, you need to know your position and that of your workplace in relation to the law. Ask to see your organisation's Equal Opportunities policy. Other key documents might include a Mission Statement and a Student Charter. There might also be a statement about curriculum and assessment entitlement.

If you approach your library they will be able to show you summaries of the main provisions of certain key Acts of Parliament, such as The Sex Discrimination Act, The Race Relations Act, The Disabled Persons Act, The Children Act and The Data Protection Act.

If you are in a college or training centre you will probably find a designated member of staff to advise you on learners' rights, your responsibilities and sources of help you can draw on. An academic head or training manager will be able to tell you about appeals and grievance procedures to protect individual rights to fair systems of learning and assessment. The awarding bodies also have equal opportunity and appeals policies and procedures. If you are preparing to take either or both of the units D32 and D33 of the Vocational Assessor's Award, you will need to explore the policies followed in your workplace to prevent discrimination in learning and assessment.

You can also refer to the Health, Safety and Welfare at Work Act to make sure that your learners, particularly anyone with a disability, are in a safe learning environment.

Taking a positive approach

What do you do if one of your group abuses another in racist language in one of your sessions, or if a sub-group of a larger class is afraid to come to lessons because they fear harassment? The solutions depend partly on your organisation's guidelines, which you should know, but it is worth working out some strategies of your own. One of the most useful approaches is to develop a set of ground rules with your group.

Establishing ground rules

Ground rules are a set of rules which you negotiate with a group of learners in the early stages of a programme or course. They are a code of conduct which is created and maintained by the group. Those who step outside them are letting the **group** down. This is a problem for the group and they must deal with the infringement. It is useful to negotiate the sanctions at the same time as the rules.

ACTIVITY

Work out a set of rules which you would like if you were a learner. Then think how you could introduce a similar exercise to the next group with whom you will be working.

Here is a set or rules created by a young adult group for use in their communication skills lessons.

Ground Rules for Fair Treatment in this Group

(1) No one should be called names because of colour, race, gender or background.

(2) We all listen if someone wants to tell us how they do things in their country or culture.

(3) We don't refer to groups of people as if they were all the same, such as women, young people.

(4) We don't refer to people carrying out traditional roles as if they were the only ones to do it, such as women cooking, or men playing football.

(5) We don't make jokes about people with problems they can't do anything about, such as being lame or blind.

(6) We don't tell racist jokes, such as about the Irish.

(7) We let everyone have a turn at speaking if they want to.

(8) If anyone joins this group who needs help with anything physical we will all take turns in helping.

Another approach to equal opportunities is to get together with other staff, perhaps as a course or programme team, and examine every aspect of the programme you offer to see if it truly reflects the interests of all the learners. You might find it helpful to make yourselves a checklist of questions so that you proceed systematically. The example which follows might be a starting point for you.

Thinking about equal opportunities: some questions you can ask about the programme on which you work

1. *Marketing* – Do we know what our learners really need? Who has decided this, and on what basis?

2. *Publicity* – Do we reach the people who would benefit? How could we get in touch?

3. *Access* – Can potential learners reach us? Is the course at the right place and time? What changes would help them attend?

4. *Enrolment* – Are there barriers at this stage? How do we change this?

5. *Content* – Is it relevant and meaningful to the students? Do the learners have a say in what is studied?

6. *Methods* – Do our teaching and learning strategies suit our learners? How could we adapt or vary them?

7. *Materials* – Are the teaching and learning aids motivating? Do they put any learners off in any way?

8. *Assessment* – Are our ways of checking learning fair to all our learners? How could we adapt them?
9. *Support* – What can we offer those of our learners who need extra support in or out of class? Where can we get help from if we need it?
10. *Staff* – Are the right people working with these students? Are they good role models? What kind of support do they need to do their work?
11. *Language* – Are we communicating at the right level? How can we check we are using appropriate styles?
12. *Ethos* – Is ours a welcoming environment where learners feel at home? What else could we do to help students feel they belong?

Helping students with learning difficulties and disabilities

If you are working with students who have learning difficulties such as dyslexia or poor numeracy, or those who have disabilities such as visual or hearing impairment, you will need to take their particular circumstances into account at all stages of their learning and assessment. Begin by talking to them about what they feel would help them. They can probably help you draw up a list of guidelines for yourself.

You will want to ensure that they have the right to the same quality of learning and assessment as other learners and are not disadvantaged by any of the circumstances. You may find it helpful to take advice also from specialist staff, or to sit in on activities run by more experienced teachers.

Your students need to feel at ease in the surroundings; this may mean inviting them in to get the feel of the place before the session starts. Ask them if seating, equipment and layout are suitable. Check whether a trip to the toilet would help. Do you need to open windows for asthma sufferers?

Think about the materials you will be using. Does written material need to be enlarged? Should you read out instructions as well as write them? Could you offer your student a tape to play before or after the lesson? Where should you stand so that lip readers can follow you? Do you need to speak slowly for those with hesitant English?

Don't forget that many examination bodies let you make special arrangements for candidates who need extra time or resources. Check with them directly or ask your team leader or internal verifier for help.

Your main concern will be to maintain the learners' self-esteem, so do anything you can to give them confidence.

Summary

In this chapter you have begun to think about what is involved in getting the learning environment right, so that learners feel confident in choosing their study and assessment routes. You have investigated the types of learning opportunities you can offer and the support facilities which might also be needed. You have thought about the ways in which individual students differ in their motivations, learning needs and preferences for ways of learning. You now realise the importance of taking these factors into account when matching learning opportunities to learners. You have identified what is involved in creating good working relationships with students, both as individuals and in groups. Finally, but very importantly, you have considered ways of working towards equal opportunities in learning and assessment for all students.

You will be able to explore aspects of individual support, such as action planning and tutorial work, in greater detail later in the book, in Chapter 8 *Supporting the Individual Learner*.

It is now time to move to the next stage of the teaching/training cycle, to examine the business of planning for learning. In the next chapter you will see how the knowledge you have gained about your students helps you to plan the routes they can take to meet their objectives.

3 Planning for Learning

Systematic decision making

Planning is the bridge between your identification of learners' needs and the learning activities they undertake. It is a vital stage in the teaching/training cycle and deserves your full attention whether you are planning whole programmes, courses or single sessions.

Planning is the process of making decisions about the directions that learners will take and the activities they will engage in to help them meet their long- and short-term goals. It may involve negotiation with learners and other staff, and will need to be followed up by thorough preparation. Preparation is the process of organising and communicating your planning decisions. It includes briefing everyone involved in the learning process, organising accommodation, facilities and equipment, preparing teaching and learning resources, and keeping your material up to date.

Both planning and preparation call for plenty of lead time; rushed decisions and hasty preparation cause stress for both teachers and students.

This chapter deals with planning for both single sessions and complete programmes and courses. It also gives you an overview of much of the rest of the book, since a discussion of planning involves a preliminary examination of all the other stages of the teaching cycle. You may want to move to and fro between this chapter and the more specialist ones which follow – you will find many points which are introduced here are followed up in detail, particularly in the case studies which you will find in each chapter.

The need for planning

All teachers and trainers need to be able to plan learning experiences. This is a highly skilled, creative process which calls for both logical analysis and intuition. Whether you are designing all parts of a learning programme or individual sessions, or whether you are organising material other people have designed, you are involved in a creative process of problem solving. Programme and session planning are complex but satisfying activities which invite you to research and weigh up many interacting variables before making decisions.

Planning is **essential** if students are to learn successfully. They lose confidence rapidly if they cannot see the direction of their learning. They need beginnings, endings and staging posts along the way. It is all too easy for subject experts to overlook the need of novices for a carefully sequenced programme, organised according to a logic which they understand. The established practice of beginning training days with a rehearsal of the objectives, and courses with an outline of the scheme of work, is based on sound psychology. Learners are entering foreign country when they embark on new learning. At one level they need a map – practical evidence that they are in good hands. At a deeper level they need a programme which has been based on sound principles of learning, such as that new learning should be based on familiar ground.

Students are also **entitled** to properly planned programmes of learning. They are investing time, effort and money in this one life option among many. They are also investing their trust in the teaching profession and not a little of their self-esteem. One poorly planned session is unlikely to do much harm, but it does not take much unfocused activity to demotivate learners of any age, and to remind busy adults that they have many other uses for their time.

ACTIVITY

Draw up a list of the advantages of a planned framework of learning for both learners and teachers/trainers. Then compare your ideas with the suggestions which follow.

Advantages of planning

FOR STUDENTS
- creates a feeling of confidence
- shows the overall pattern
- demonstrates how the parts fit into the whole
- helps them prepare for sessions and activities
- helps them gather together any resources needed
- helps them structure study time

FOR TEACHERS/TRAINERS
- promotes a feeling of confidence
- helps you to prepare for sessions and activities
- helps you to order or prepare resources
- imposes structure on a large body of material
- keeps you focused on students' needs
- provides a structure for another teacher to follow
- sets up a framework for planning assessment
- sets up a framework for evaluating your work

In summary, planning is essential for effective learning, **provided that** you build in flexibility and that you are prepared to vary your planning when you come to actual practice. You will be examining ways to do this later in the chapter.

Your role in planning

Let's look at **your** particular role in planning. Are you involved in any of these activities?

- planning single sessions within someone else's programme, such as a dietician who gives a lecture on nutrition within a training programme for physiotherapists;

- planning the practical sessions in a programme shared with others who are responsible for teaching underpinning knowledge, such as a teacher of chiropody who supervises students' clinical practice;
- planning theory sessions for groups whose practical work is handled by other staff, such as an expert in oncology providing update briefings for Macmillan nurses;
- planning short courses for a range of organisations, such as an update of computer packages for business users;
- planning long courses for further education students, for example, BTEC Intermediate GNVQ in Hospitality and Catering;
- working with candidates for APL (Accreditation of Prior Learning) who are planning how to present evidence of competence, such as in practical hairdressing;
- planning one-day sessions to provide an introduction or further expertise in a specialist skill, such as sugarcraft or yoga;
- planning on-the-job training and assessment for an employee candidate, such as a chef seeking City & Guilds NVQ level 2 in Food Preparation and Cooking;
- adapting existing training programmes to fit a new client group, such as a First Aid programme for people with disabilities.

Whatever your role, before you can start planning you will need to gather various kinds of information. We'll go on to look at that process now.

Gathering essential information

There are four areas about which you will need information. You will need to know what is expected of you, and you will need to know about the learning programme/course, the students and the resources available. Let's investigate each of these in turn.

1. *Find out what is expected of you*

You need to know what you must produce or organise within a set timescale, and the amount of scope you have to exercise your initiative – it is always wise to check this. You will have to consult a range of people. It's a good idea to have a checklist for this task, as it is very easy for both of you to assume the other person knows more than they do. Make sure you ask about deadlines, permissions, budgets, any documentation you should read and other people you should consult.

2. *Find out about the learning programme / course*

ACTIVITY

Make a list of all the things you will need to know about the course, session or programme, such as the way the learners are assessed. Look back at the list of different situations in the previous section (*Your role in planning*) to help you think of several different contexts.

Here are some of the areas you will need to find out about; you probably had many more items of your own.

- the purpose of the course, its aims, objectives and outcomes, whether it deals with practical performance or underpinning knowledge and understanding, or both;
- the way the course is structured, if it is modular or unit based or in stages, if there is work experience;
- how any assessment is organised, if it is continuous or at the end, if it is by portfolios of evidence or by assignments or examinations;
- the level, amount and weighting of the material and the pace at which the students are expected to go;
- the style of teaching and learning expected by staff and students;
- organisational factors and constraints, including the duration of the course and of sessions, their frequency and pattern, and the availability of resources.

As you can see, planning is not an isolated activity; you will need to talk to all manner of teaching and support staff in order to make your decisions. If your course is the kind which is planned **with** rather than **for** the learners, you will be able to plan an outline and various options which you can then negotiate with the group when you meet. It is important to have worked out what is feasible **before** you meet the students.

3.   *Find out about the learners/students*

You have already thought about getting to know your students in the previous chapter, *Getting Started*. A glance back will remind you of the facts you need as the basis for your planning, whether you are working on a single session or a complete programme. You will need to ask:

- how many of them are there?
- what is their age, gender and cultural background?
- what are their present levels of ability?
- what have they studied already?
- what other relevant experiences have they had?
- what kinds of motivation do they have?
- what learning and support needs do they have?

The information you gather will offer you both opportunities and constraints. In some cases students will all be from the same professional group with similar abilities and expectations. Other groups may have a wide range of abilities and learning background. The nature of the programme and its particular context can also affect your choices; if the style of learning is unfamiliar to the students you will have to go more slowly and carefully than in an area where everyone knows what to expect. As you can see, planning has to take into account not just the nature of the course and the nature of the students **but the way these two groups of factors interact**.

4.   *Find out about the resources*

You have already considered in the previous chapter the importance of getting the learning environment right. When you plan you have to take into account practical considerations to do with accommodation and facilities, as well as the availability of suitable teaching aids and learning resources. Let's look first at the physical environment.

Many a course, short or long, has been successful or problematic because of the rooms it is in. Too many groups spend hours learning in rooms without natural light. You may have very little choice or none, but it is helpful to have a picture of the accommodation you would like so that you can negotiate clearly for it.

ACTIVITY

Use your imagination or experience to suggest the kind of learning environment which these teachers would try to arrange for their groups:

(1) John, teaching yoga to an adult evening class;
(2) Juliet, teaching A-level theatre studies to 16–19-year-olds;
(3) Fran, teaching self-help cookery to adults with disabilities;
(4) Kate, training revenue protection officers in customer care.

Here are some suggestions:

John – he needs a large room without furniture, with good ventilation, lights which can be dimmed, a warm floor covering, a power point for a tape recorder, space for storing piles of mats, in an area free of noise or interruptions.

Juliet – she needs a large space with only a little flexible furniture for practical sessions, space to store props and materials, good ventilation, theatre lighting, window blinds or curtains, sound proofing or distance from other rooms.

Fran – she needs a purpose-built kitchen on the ground floor with wheelchair access to the room and within it. She needs well spaced out work stations so that learners and helpers can work side by side. All the storage facilities need to be clearly labelled with their contents. She needs good ventilation and quiet surroundings. A whiteboard would be useful for illustrations. All her facilities and equipment need to be in full working order.

Kate – she needs a room large enough for simulation work in which she can use a video camera and play-back facilities. She needs good ventilation, adjustable lighting and possibly sound proofing.

As you can see, all the teachers need appropriate ventilation, space and lighting. Some need specialist equipment, all need storage areas and flexible furniture. They may also need a whiteboard or flip chart, overhead projector and screen, and the space to position these appropriately for viewing.

You will find it helpful when you are planning to think about the surroundings in this degree of detail. If possible go and look at the area where you will be working. This may motivate you to some remedial action **before** the event.

Teaching aids and learning resources

Many teaching and training organisations have resource centres, library and IT facilities which can be used by students and teachers. You should be able to find a leaflet describing them and the opening hours. There may also be support staff whose role is to help with difficulties, such as in an open access computing area. You may be surprised at the range of materials available, especially if they have been able to install an open learning suite with multimedia facilities. You may need to arrange training for yourself and your students to use some of the resources. Don't assume students will be familiar with the resources, they would probably benefit from an induction to both the library services and the technology (see Figure 3.1).

Designing courses and programmes

Now let's get down to the detailed business of planning. You have gathered all the information you can and you know what is expected of you. You will follow a very similar process whether you are planning for a course or for a single session. Some people prefer to begin with the larger picture, the course, then go on to the smaller activity, the lesson. This is what we are going to do now in this chapter. If you would prefer, turn to the later part of the chapter on planning single sessions, then come back to this section when you are ready.

◀ **Figure 3.1**
Self-directed study in an open-learning centre.

When you design a course or programme you have to consider a number of component parts. These are:

- the course aims;
- the learning objectives/outcomes;
- the content (subject matter);
- the teaching and learning strategies (methods);
- the teaching aids and learning resources;
- methods of monitoring and reviewing learning;
- methods of assessing achievement;
- the way you will evaluate the course.

You will be able to work through each of these in a moment, but first you might like to carry out a small exercise in course design.

ACTIVITY

You will gain more from this activity if you can do it with a colleague.

Safety and security in the home

Design a 10 × 2 hour short course of this title. Make decisions about time, venue, content, sequence of topics, teaching and learning methods, ways of assessing learning and evaluation of the course. You do not have a large budget. The course aims are already stated. They are:

> **To alert you to the range of hazards present in the home and to advise you on preventing harm to people and property.**

The students have already been recruited. The class list includes:

- a woman in her 50s, recently widowed
- two single parents
- a school caretaker nearing retirement
- a career woman living on her own
- two students living in rented rooms
- a librarian caring for both elderly parents
- a housewife lacking fluent English
- a Girl Guide captain
- a secretary of a *Neighbourhood Watch* scheme.

You might find it helpful to use a layout such as the one shown in Figure 3.2. The main headings will apply to all your sessions, the information in the columns will vary for each specific session.

COURSE PLANNING OUTLINE

Course Title

Level, e.g. Introductory, Intermediate, Advanced

Number and duration of sessions

◀ **Figure 3.2**
A useful planning format (continued on page 26).

Course meeting time

Number of participants   Age range

Venue

Ways of checking learning

Course aims

Session Number	Session Title	Session Objectives	Main Activities	Resources

◀ **Figure** 3.2
(continued)

What did you decide? You probably tried to suit the class mix in your choice of time, venue, course content, choice of teaching methods and forms of assessment. You had to make assumptions about their needs from the bare facts given – this is the reality for many teachers, they adjust their plans after the first session when they have met the participants.

You probably used the course aims to decide that the course is introductory level and has a double focus, **alert** and **prevent**. This and the group mix will have helped you decide which topics to include and how much time to give each. You will have used a particular logic in choosing the sequence of topics, maybe going round the house room by room, maybe categorising the hazards by age group (babies, older people) or type of danger (electricity, water). You would have used the course aims (advise) and group (adults) to choose methods such as instruction and demonstration, possibly using a variety of visual aids to help everyone but particularly the student with hesitant English. Maybe you encouraged the more knowledgeable ones (Guide captain, caretaker) to play an active part? You may have decided formal assessment was not appropriate to this group, but you would have consulted them for the evaluation.

Carry these ideas with you, as you now examine in turn each of the course components you saw listed earlier in the chapter.

Formulating aims and objectives

An aim is a general statement of the overall direction of the course. It tells you what the teacher will intend to achieve. It does not tell you how to achieve it – this is what you work out in your planning. Aims are usually specified for the whole course or programme, and then for individual parts of it. They tend in both cases to be long-term broad statements which need to be translated into more immediate terms. Here are two examples:

‘To prepare trainees for a range of roles in the leisure industry.’
‘To enable participants to become familiar with the structure, functions and applications of a range of computer languages.’

These are signposts only; you now need to break down the general concept into a session by session plan, working out aims and objectives for each session.

Individual lesson aims are also quite broad and based on what the **teacher** intends to do. Here are some examples from a group of teachers to whom we will refer throughout this chapter; later in this section you can see the objectives which they devised to put these aims into action.

Graham, teaching IT Fundamentals
'To revise binary to decimal and decimal to binary conversions'

Hilary, teaching Food Hygiene
'To introduce the causes of food poisoning and methods of prevention'

Diane, teaching Physiotherapy
'To demonstrate and give practice in techniques of subjective examination for patients with musculoskeletal disorders'

Gerry, teaching Child Development
'To give information on the growth and development of a baby to six months'

Some of these statements give you more help than others in seeing how the lesson might develop, but all of them need to be turned into specific statements of what the **students** will be able to achieve, that is into objectives, before you can plan any further.

Learning objectives are statements of what learners should be capable of doing **after** a period of learning. Don't be confused by the use of the world objective in everyday conversation, where it means much the same as aims. In an educational context, objectives are precise descriptions of how you want the learner to be able to perform or behave as a result of successful learning. Objectives are always expressed from the point of view of the learner. Now look carefully at some examples which match the lesson aims of the teachers quoted above.

Graham, teaching IT Fundamentals
At the end of the lesson the students will be able to:
- convert binary numbers to decimal;
- convert decimal numbers to binary;
- explain the need for such conversions in practice.

Hilary, teaching Food Hygiene
The students will be able to:
- describe the symptoms of food poisoning;
- name the causes of food poisoning;
- describe the conditions in which bacteria thrive;
- identify ten sources of food poisoning on a diagram provided;
- list three ways of reducing the risk of food poisoning.

Diane, teaching Subjective Examination Techniques in Physiotherapy
The trainee physiotherapist will:
- put the patient at their ease before questioning;
- question in a logical sequence;
- listen attentively to responses;
- mark the patient's symptoms accurately on a body chart.

Gerry, teaching Child Development
Students will be able to:

- identify the key stages of a baby's development;
- talk to a mother about her baby's development;
- gather information from this session for an assignment.

What did you notice about these objectives?

- they are specific, for instance, ten sources of food poisoning;
- they refer to activity which can be seen and heard;
- they begin with a verb, such as name, describe, identify;
- they use simple sentence structures and plain language (except for specialist terms which students must learn);
- they provide the 'bones' of the lesson;
- they cover different areas of learning, for example
  - knowledge and understanding – explain, discuss
  - skills – talk to a mother, question in a logical sequence
  - attitudes – listen attentively;
- they set targets for the students to achieve;
- they could form the basis of formal assessment;
- they provide the teacher with evidence of learning, mostly within the lesson itself;
- they could help the teacher evaluate the effectiveness of their teaching – has the lesson helped the students to achieve their targets?

You can see from these examples that objectives are easy to specify for all kinds of subject area and provide a good guide to the content of the lessons, to your choice of teaching and learning strategies and to the content of your assessment.

ACTIVITY

Create a set of objectives for the next session which you intend to teach. Discuss them with a colleague if possible.

Were you sufficiently precise? Were you tempted to use general phrases such as 'the student will understand'? If so, ask yourself how you will **know** that the student understands. You have probably asked in class, 'Does everyone understand?' and received lots of assenting nods and murmurs. Yet when you check this, by asking students to explain the concept back to you, you find that they have not grasped the ideas fully.

The best way for you and the students to be sure of their understanding is to make them demonstrate it, as they would a physical skill. You can ask them within the lesson to explain or describe a process, or you can give them follow-on tasks to prove their understanding. Your objectives need to specify that they will 'state' or 'identify' or 'describe', not just that they will 'know' or 'understand', for example

'The students will be able to **explain** the concept of customer care and **give four examples** from the work of staff in the Hospitality Industry' is more helpful than

'The students will understand the concept of customer care'

Outcomes

Learners working towards NVQ and GNVQ qualifications are aiming to match their own performance to a very detailed specification of what competence at a particular level in a given vocational area would look like. This specification is already laid down in the documentation which teachers and learners receive from the awarding bodies. These outcomes relate to the end result of a whole period of learning, whether you have learned on a course or at work or at home. The outcome is, therefore, the standard which learners must meet. It forms an assessment specification which is used to check their level of competence.

Objectives refer to particular lessons, are not as detailed as outcomes and are usually devised by you or negotiated between you and your group, when you are planning each session. They are not an assessment specification in their own right, but act as your guide when you are devising suitable forms of assessment for your students.

Deciding on content

As you have seen, the objectives give you the framework for the session and lead you to the choice of content or subject matter. One of the most difficult decisions in planning is what to include, followed by how much of it to include. Let's look at this first from the viewpoint of a whole course, then go on to look at individual sessions.

Your first task is to use the course guidelines, aims or outcomes to decide on topic areas to include, then to estimate the pace at which learners will be able to deal with them – this helps you to decide on the amount to include. If you are working on an NVQ or GNVQ programme you will have to include everything. If you are working to a GCSE or A-level syllabus the subject areas will be prescribed, although you may have some choices. You may decide to cover certain areas in set sessions but ask students to research other areas on their own under your guidance.

The amount of importance which you give to different sections of the subject material, usually shown by the amount of time you allocate to it, is known as **weighting** (see Figure 3.3). How you weight your subject material will depend on several other factors besides the objectives. These include:

- what the students want out of the course – adults on non-certificated courses would expect to have a say;
- what you know from experience students find difficult and need more time on;
- what you know employers want (sometimes awarding body requirements are out of date);
- what previous assessment papers suggest are favourite topics;
- what your course team or workplace thinks is important.

The advantage of working out beforehand the right balance of time for topics (and communicating these to students in a written scheme of work) is that it makes you stick to the plan rather than following your own interests and preferences. It is all too easy to linger over areas **you** enjoy, perhaps to the detriment of the students' objectives.

◄ **Figure 3.3**
Weighting takes careful thought.

One way of making your decisions is to ask yourself three questions:

What **must** the students know?
What **should** the students know?
What **could** the students know?

'Know' in this context also means 'do' and 'experience', it covers all three areas of learning, knowing and understanding, skills and attitude development. 'Must' also implies that you have consulted students in those cases where you are able to negotiate course content, it is a shared 'must' between you and the learners.

Now regard these questions as representing three concentric circles, as in Figure 3.4. You might find it helpful to draw the circles on a large piece of flip chart paper. Put 'must' in the centre, 'should' in the second circle and 'could' on the outside. Then make your decisions. The 'could' category is all those aspects which it would be good to include if there was lots of time, but which the students could research themselves.

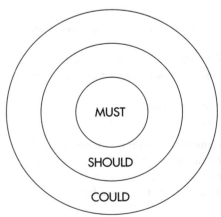

◄ **Figure 3.4**
Deciding on content.

You can follow this process to decide the content of a whole course, a unit or module or a single session.

Setting the level and pace

Your estimate of how the students can cope in a given time will have to be an informed guess until you get to know them better. Even then you may be wrong, since every group is different. New teachers are often over-ambitious about the amount of information or activity which will go into a session. You forget that you are an expert in the subject, and you find it difficult to imagine how much slower a novice can be at grasping the point. Students need lots of practice and revision. You will find that giving over the first 15 minutes of any session to a review of the main points of the previous one will be time well spent.

Pace of work is connected to the level of work expected of the students, the level which you have to help them to match. You will probably find that the students are at a different level from that which you expect, and from each other. Most classes in further and adult education are mixed in their abilities, even if there is a set of entry requirements. You will need to plan for this within the lessons as well as arranging appropriate help outside. When you draw up your course plans, try to leave yourself 'recovery time' to cater for those who need longer than expected. It is never a good idea to commit every session fully.

Determining the sequence of material

There are lots of ways of ordering the learning material. Your first ideas will probably come from the ways you yourself like to learn.

ACTIVITY

Brainstorm several different ways of organising subject matter; decide which would suit your field of work. Here are some suggestions:

(1) By the logic of the subject – what must have precedence, for instance the pronunciation patterns of a foreign language before its grammar, or the present tense of a verb before the past tense;

(2) By ease of learning – easier before harder, such as arithmetic before algebra, simple verbs before compound verbs;

(3) Chronologically – in order of event or development, such as the history of art, fashion, literature;

(4) By themes – according to a pattern which occurs in different contexts or periods, such as the treatment of children, money or death in the literature of different countries;

(5) By issues – a series of significant areas, such as the sea, food, land use in environmental studies;

(6) By processes – different methods or skills, such as boiling, grilling, baking in catering;

(7) By need to know – immediacy of need, such as floating in swimming, lesson planning in teacher training;

(8) Spirally – two or more visits to each area of content at increasing levels of complexity, such as listening skills in counselling;

(9) Mimicry – sequencing material in the way you were taught, copying someone else's model;

(10) Pragmatically – as and when the need arises, such as training on the job when a particular need becomes apparent.

As you can see, there are many ways to approach your subject area. You might like to consider changing from your established approach if you think the change will make the material more meaningful for the students.

Choosing teaching and learning strategies

Think back to the ideas you had for teaching on the short course *Safety and Security in the Home*. Did they include any of the following strategies?

- giving information/presentations, such as on fire hazards;
- demonstrating, for instance, how to give First Aid;
- discussion, such as what to do first in an emergency;
- exercises, such as identifying danger areas in a kitchen;
- talks by visiting experts, such as the police;
- making a visit, for example, to a home safety exhibition.

If you had had more time you might have added:

- setting a project, such as researching security lights;
- role play, such as dealing with an intruder;
- practical session, such as security-marking possessions;
- case studies, for instance, analysing reasons for a fire outbreak;
- tutorials, for example, advising confidentially on individual situations.

The point of this list is to show how many interesting and relevant ways there are to meet the learning objectives.

As you read further in this book you will find a great deal of information about teaching and training methods, including giving presentations, explaining information, instructing, giving demonstrations, coaching, organising practical lessons, using role play and simulations, case studies and exercises in small groups, and more. At the **planning** stage it is most important to decide which strategies will be the most effective in helping your students learn. These may not be the ones which **you** would prefer to learn from, nor the ones you most enjoy using, but they must be the ones the students need. The emphasis in the rest of this section is on the factors which will influence your decisions. For detailed descriptions of the methods themselves, turn to Chapter 5 *Presenting Information and Ideas*, Chapter 6 *Organising Learning in Groups* and Chapter 7 *Teaching a Skill*.

Choosing the right approach

You will base your decisions on two main factors, the demands of the objectives and the students' preferences. You noticed in Chapter 2 *Getting Started* that learners may have preconceived ideas about ways of learning. Some adults, for example, might expect to be lectured at. They may feel that group work or role play are not real learning because they seem informal and don't include taking notes. You will probably find a range of attitudes, positive and negative, in most groups. It will be up to you to show the students the point of the methods chosen; they need to know how what they are asked to do will help them achieve their goals.

You can divide teaching and learning strategies into three main groups according to their usefulness in achieving a particular purpose. This may help you to decide which ones are best for your teaching situation. The categories are:

    Presentation
    Interaction
    Search

Presentation methods are those in which an expert, often the teacher, provides a great deal of information and ideas. Typically the speaker dominates the session, although they may encourage questions and comment. They often use teaching aids such as the overhead projector, and students are likely to take notes. There is relatively little interaction with or between students and limited opportunities to check learning.

Interaction methods imply frequent contributions by students, work in small groups where they share ideas and produce materials, an active approach to learning and plenty of opportunity to check learning there and then.

Search strategies are those where students are briefed before acting on their own responsibility to find and research information and ideas. They use libraries and resource centres and often leave the buildings where they are based. Later they receive feedback on their learning.

ACTIVITY

Make a list under these three headings of all the teaching and learning strategies/methods you have experienced or heard of which seem to you to answer the descriptions above.
   Here are some suggestions:

Presentation
- lecture (sometimes called exposition), talk
- demonstration
- dictation, such as notetaking
- showing a film, slides or video.

Interaction
- brainstorming (offering suggestions in a large group)
- discussion
- questioning
- practical
- buzz group (discussion in pairs)
- exercises in small groups
- case studies (discussing solutions to problem situations)
- simulation (practising for real future situations)
- role play (acting a part to learn how it feels).

Search
- projects (researching material to answer a brief)
- experiments (practical research to discover findings)
- visits (learning from experiences in new locations)
- case study (finding the data to help solve the problem).

Don't think that these approaches occur in isolation from each other. You can devise interesting and creative combinations within and between categories, if they are justified by the lesson aims. This is all part of the excitement and satisfaction of planning for learning.

ACTIVITY

Look back at the group of teachers whose aims and objectives you examined earlier in the chapter. What do you think would be the most suitable strategies for them to use to enable their students to meet their stated objectives?

Your list might include these suggestions:

Graham (IT)
- instruction + demonstration, to show the process to follow;
- practical, to allow the students to do it for themselves;
- questioning, to check on understanding of principles.

Hilary (Food Hygiene)
- instruction + explanation, to give the facts;
- questioning, to check understanding;
- small group exercise, to complete the diagram.

Diane (Physiotherapy)
- simulation + role play to practise interpersonal skills;
- individual exercise, to complete chart;
- questioning, to check understanding.

Gerry (Child Development)
- explaining + research, to provide the underpinning knowledge;
- questioning, to check understanding;
- practical investigation, to explore the real situation.

You will have noticed how often questioning is included to check that the other strategies have been successful. As you now move on to plan your own teaching and learning strategies, bear in mind a few additional but significant points:

- **always** explain to your students why you are using the methods; what is obvious to you may be very unclear to them;
- make it clear to the students that they have indeed met the objectives; this may not be apparent, for example, from role play;
- check that the methods you use do not put any of the learners at a disadvantage; be sure the activities are justified by the objectives and explain this. If anyone has difficulties, you will need to offer extra support, for instance, students whose first language is not English may find full group discussion intimidating, so start with pair work and small group discussion.

Deciding on teaching aids and learning resources

You will find a full discussion of this area in Chapter 4 *Teaching Aids and Learning Resources* following on from this chapter. This section introduces those factors which you need to consider when you are engaged in planning.

Thinking about aids and resources goes hand in hand with thinking about teaching and learning strategies, in fact it is easy to confuse the two areas. Strategies refer to **activities**, such as putting learners into small groups to carry out discussion. Aids and resources refer to **things**, such as overhead projectors and flip charts, and to **people**, such as other students, staff in the workplace or the teacher/trainer.

Teaching aids are objects, materials and equipment used by the teacher/trainer to help them illustrate their explanations and get the point across. They include chalkboards, whiteboards and flip charts; overhead projectors (the machine) and overhead transparencies (pieces or roll of acetate used with them); computer hardware and software; slide and film projectors; video machines and videos; visual materials such as charts, photographs and pictures; static or working models; real objects and equipment.

Learning resources are materials, objects or people used by learners to help them to study and learn. They include books, slides and films, audio and video tapes, computer programs, work sheets and work books, graphic materials such as photographs and illustrations, and structured experiences which may or may not involve interacting with people.

Some objects can be both teaching aids and learning resources; it depends on who has control over their use. Is the teacher showing the slides with a planned commentary or are the students consulting the slides themselves to extract information for a project? Typical resource-based learning strategies are projects, where the teacher guides the students towards the resources which will help them meet the project brief, but the students then work on their own with the resources to extract what they need.

There are some questions you will need to ask yourself when planning to use aids and resources. They include:

- how will the materials improve the students' learning opportunities?
- do I have access to the aids and resources I need?
- have I the right accommodation and facilities to use them?
- have I time in the session(s) to use them properly?
- do I or the students need training to use the materials? have I time to arrange this?
- will my choice of materials disadvantage anyone in the group;
- what is the cost? can I afford it?

Planning to monitor and review learning

You can read in detail about these activities in Chapter 8 *Supporting the Individual Learner*. Here at the planning stage you need to think about creating time for them within your learning programme or scheme of work, and choosing the right timing to be most helpful to your students/trainees.

Monitoring progress is an activity which can only be carried out over time. You have to judge how much teaching and learning have to go on before it is appropriate to set up an individual or group tutorial to check how learners are progressing. You may want to do this outside the taught programme, or within part of each session, or as a separate session at regular intervals. You may prefer to set individual learners their own timetable for review, or to have all members of a group 'report in' at a given time. Your decisions will be related to the pace of learning your students can achieve.

The right timing for review is hard to estimate; you will get a feel for this as you get to know your learners better.

You would be wise to leave some space in the overall programme or scheme for consolidating learning, in case you find during your monitoring and review that students need more teaching or practice.

Integrating assessment

You can examine assessment practices in detail in Chapter 9, *Assessing Achievement*. For the moment it is important to realise that you must plan assessment into your course and individual sessions from the beginning. This is true whether you assess in a formal or less formal manner. In one sense learning is an end in itself, but most learners want to know to what extent they have achieved their learning objectives, in order to experience satisfaction or to renew their efforts.

You may be working on a programme where the assessment regime is set by an awarding body, such as City & Guilds or the RSA Examinations Board NVQ and GNVQ schemes. Or you may have control over what, when and how you assess. Whatever your situation, you need to think about preparation for assessment, the assessment itself and the feedback on results which you will give afterwards. Each of these stages requires your thorough attention, and will be taken very seriously by your students.

Ways of carrying out assessment

There are lots of ways in which you can check on your students learning, from questioning in the session itself to formal examinations.

Your choice will depend on the nature of your course, the expectations of the students and practical considerations such as the amount of time available. For instance, a short answer test will fit into a one-hour session but you may need two sessions for a presentation by all members of a class.

ACTIVITY

What kinds of assessment do you think the first three teachers whom you met earlier in the chapter have chosen for their students? Make suggestions which seem to you to suit their objectives.

Graham, teaching IT Fundamentals to full-time college students, has decided to start each of the ten sessions with a short answer written test to make sure that they can do the basics. They will mark each other's papers and have immediate feedback. This will take 30 minutes each week.

Hilary, teaching Food Hygiene to volunteers in a community setting, does not use formal assessment. She will set them a practical cookery task after four sessions and observe them in action. She will ask them questions while she does so. This will take the whole session. She will give feedback at the time to the whole group.

Diane, teaching Physiotherapy to trainees, will test their underpinning knowledge in a written test in one of her 2-hour sessions after 4 weeks. She will brief them on what to expect in the previous session and give them full feedback in the one which follows.

It may help you to plan assessment systematically if you think of it as having several stages. Depending on your situation you may be involved in all or some of these:

(1) devising tests (and trying them out – piloting them – to see if they are suitable);
(2) preparing learners to be assessed;
(3) collecting evidence of the learners' degree of competence and achievement;
(4) making judgements about the evidence, for example, have they reached the standard?
(5) giving learners feedback on their achievement.

You will need to allow time for all these stages.

Equally important is the timing of assessment. If you work on a modular or unit-based scheme you may have to test at set intervals. If you run an integrated course you can plan assignments throughout the programme, spaced to take account of your particular group. This kind of planning takes practice, like any other teacher skill.

Building in evaluation

The final component of the learning programme is its evaluation. A major responsibility of all teachers is to look back over their teaching at regular intervals and judge the degree of their effectiveness. This applies whether you work on whole programmes or single sessions, and whatever the setting. The extent to which you can include your students in this evaluation will vary, but you should always try to consult them.

Again there are several ways in which you can carry out evaluation. This topic is covered very thoroughly towards the end of the book in Chapter 10 *Evaluation*. At this planning stage you are again thinking about the need to build into your scheme occasions to involve the students in discussion and feedback on the way they have been taught. These can be lively occasions, far more interesting than the mere filling in of the predictable evaluation form. The lessons **you** learn from the evaluation will, of course, be the basis of your planning for your next course or session.

Pulling the threads together

This has been a lengthy discussion, of necessity since planning involves thinking about all the stages of the teaching cycle. There are just two more points to make before we move on to look at planning individual sessions. They are the need for **coherence** and **flexibility** in your scheme.

Coherence is all about helping students to see the whole picture. This is often difficult for them, as they do not already know the whole area of study as you do, and they are covering it in small sections. Your students need to be able to see a clear purpose and a sense of direction in their learning. They need to appreciate the links between the sections and to have a sense of arriving at their goal. There are many ways you can help them; here are just three. You could:

- give them a diagram at the beginning which shows how all the parts fit together;
- relate every session to the course aims and objectives;
- develop assignments which bring aspects of the course together even if they are taught separately.

Flexibility is perhaps the most important teacher skill/attitude of all. You need to be prepared to make changes to any part of your planning and activities. The behaviour of students, other staff, mechanical objects and equipment cannot be predicted with certainty and 'flu and bad weather can play havoc with the best planned scheme.

Flexibility is a response to good news as well as bad, to unexpected opportunities for your students as well as to problems. You may want to take advantage of a visiting expert or a chance of work experience, or you may have to give extra time to revision if you find that students have not coped well with a particular topic.

The secret of flexibility is to leave spaces in your planning rather than to commit all your time, and to have contingency plans for those events which you can reasonably predict may happen. You could build up your bank of possible solutions by talking to more experienced staff about their responses to problem situations.

Finally, let's summarise the characteristics of an effective programme of work. You could use these points as a checklist. Your course programme should:

- cover the course aims and objectives;
- be at the right level and pace for the students;
- prepare learners for assessment (if appropriate);
- have an overall design which can be explained simply;
- provide a variety of activities to keep learners motivated;
- follow a logical sequence;
- have built-in review time;
- be flexible.

Designing individual sessions

A great deal of what has been said about planning courses applies to planning individual sessions or lessons, but on a smaller scale. You will need to consider:

- the lesson aims and objectives;
- the choice of content, its amount and level;
- the choice of teaching and learning strategies;
- appropriate teaching aids and learning resources;
- suitable ways of checking learning;
- the order of events in the lesson;
- contingency plans.

Many students, when asked what they want from lessons, say:

- clear objectives whose relevance is explained;
- plenty of activity;

- opportunities to ask questions;
- the right level and pace.

Plans and formats

You will need a lesson plan. This can be a single sheet of paper on which you sketch out the stages of the lesson, the amount of time allocated to each, the activities you and the students will engage in, and the resources you will need. It is best headed up with the lesson title, date, time and venue, details of the learning group and the lesson objectives.

The lesson plan is not the place for your lesson notes; you will find it easier to have these nearby on a separate sheet or set of file cards. You need to be able to see your lesson plan at a glance, so you do not want too much detail and you do need bold, clear writing. You could spread the plan over two sheets. This would be very helpful information for anyone who needed to stand in for you if you were absent or unavailable unexpectedly.

Two examples of formats you could use are shown in Figures 3.5 and 3.6.

ACTIVITY | Take either the one-sheet (Figure 3.5) or the two-sheet (Figure 3.6) lesson plan and draft a plan for a lesson you intend to give. You would find it helpful to discuss this with a colleague.

Timing

All teachers find it difficult to estimate the exact timing of a lesson, you can only give an approximate guide. You can help yourself by not being too rigid; divide the session into 15-minute rather than 5-minute blocks. There are far too many variables in classroom interaction to be more precise than this.

One ploy is to design a plan with 'options', that is, sections you can put in or leave out depending on how the lesson is evolving. This will enable you to cope with the unexpected, whether it is the discovery that the group has already covered part of this topic with another teacher or that they are ignorant of the basic topic on which your lesson depends.

Careful timing can also be thrown by changes in the students' pattern of learning. They may slow up for several reasons. They may reach a **plateau** in their learning after climbing steadily up the learning curve for a while.

It is as if the learning needed time to settle and to be assimilated before they can go on. This is quite normal. They may be suffering from overload, especially if they are studying several new subjects at once, or they may simply be slow in gathering confidence. When it comes they will progress again rapidly.

There is also the factor of 'productive time'. In any given learning hour there are times when students lose concentration. This is why experienced teachers change the activity every 15 minutes or so, the average concentration time for many learners. They will also tell you that the first 10 minutes is vital listening time, followed by a drop in attention unless students are active. Attention picks up when a new activity is introduced, and towards the end of the session. You need to plan accordingly.

LESSON PLAN

Course details   Date and time

Lesson topic

Learning objectives

Timing	Content	Students' Activity	Teacher's Activity	Aids

Means of checking learning

Contingency plan

▲ Figure 3.5
A one-page lesson plan.

LESSON PLAN

Date and time of session

Venue

Course title

Learning group (name, title, code etc.)

Number in group   Age range

Distinguishing features of group (age, gender, ethnicity)

Lesson title

Place of this session in the course

Students' previous experience/knowledge of the topic

▲ **Figure 3.6**
A two-page format (continued on page 42).

Prerequisites (what students must know before the lesson)

Lesson aims

Lesson objectives

Means of checking learning

Timing	Content	Students' Activity	Teacher's Activity	Resources	Notes

Contingency plans

▲ **Figure 3.6**
A two–page format (continued).

Starting and finishing

Effective beginnings and endings to sessions are an art in themselves. You can use these prime learning times productively rather than waste them on matters of secondary importance.

Suggest effective ways of using the first and last 10 minutes of your lesson time. Here are some suggestions.

Starting the lesson/session
- explain the aims and objectives;
- show how the material relates to the rest of the course or to activities at work;
- describe the format of the lesson, what learners will be doing;
- revise key points from a previous session;
- check your assumptions about expected knowledge.

In fact, don't launch immediately into the first topic but use this time to give a sense of purpose and organisation to the material which then follows.

Finishing the lesson/session
- summarise the points which you want everyone to remember;
- write up key points;
- tell the group which objectives they have achieved;
- give praise and encouragement;
- clarify any details of assignment work or homework;
- describe the topic of the next session.

It is worth noting some of these activities on your plan so that you build them into your timing.

Sessions which are difficult to plan

You may hear people say that you can't plan sessions which involve mainly practical work or those in which students attend a drop-in workshop to work individually with a tutor. What they probably mean is that they can't specify in neat 15-minute intervals exactly what will be happening, because the session is less under their direct control than the traditional theory or demonstration session.

Planning for a practical session

In fact, if you teach a practical subject such as catering or hairdressing you are performing tremendous feats of planning. You are estimating the time needed for comparative novices to carry out a range of tasks working with particular equipment or members of the public, all with due regard for health and safety, **and** ensuring that everything is cleared away ready for the next users of the facilities. You do have a lesson plan, but it is in your head. You are guided in part by the timing of the physical processes involved in, say, perming or grilling, in part by your understanding of the students' abilities. You can tell to the minute when the group can be allowed to relax or must move on.

You would probably find it useful to have a written plan which begins with the objectives, then indicates which processes must be completed by a given time. Here is an example from a 2-hour GNVQ Intermediate Graphics session where Ian is helping students compile a portfolio of suggestions to show to a client in answer to a design brief.

Lesson objectives
The students will be able to complete a draft of at least two items for their portfolio, present it to the tutor for feedback and work on amendments.

0–30 minutes
Explain objectives.
Check students have the tools and materials they need.
Get them started, circulate briefly to check what stage they are at, deal with initial queries.

30–60 minutes
Monitor progress, respond to requests for help.

Half-way point
All students should have begun on their second item.

60–100 minutes
See each student (alphabetical order) for 5 minutes to give feedback on progress and agree amendments, if any.

100–120 minutes
Students finish off, clear up.
Summarise progress.
Map out work for next session.

Planning for a resource centre session

Debbie works in a learning support centre, offering help to students with English language difficulties. She has five students who come to every session and another five who come intermittently. Their difficulties range through reading, writing and speaking English. Some are native speakers, others have English as their second or third language. Their understanding and progress are all at different levels.

Debbie has created a profile sheet for each student, setting out their aims, objectives for the next six sessions and their progress to date. The record includes details of the resources they are using, such as texts, tapes, and where they have got to with them. Her lesson plan consists of notes to herself about what each student should work on in this session. She will check their current fluency with each as they arrive, and either get them started on the tasks she has identified or modify her intentions to suit their needs.

Towards the end of the session, Debbie reviews each student's progress and sets them targets for the next session. After they have left she updates her profile sheets. These records enable Debbie, and any other staff member who might have to take over from her, to keep track of the students, and of course they can be shared with the learners at any time.

Planning for an unfamiliar group

You may be wondering how to plan a session for a group you have not met before, for example, if you have been asked to give a specialist lecture on someone else's course. If this is a once only occasion you will have to combine flexibility, in responding to what you find, with self-discipline in not leaving unfinished content or activities. This is difficult, even for experienced teachers.

You will need:

- a very clear brief from the course organiser, including objectives and information about any linked assessment activities to be undertaken by the students later;
- information about the group's composition and dynamics;
- briefing about the accommodation and facilities (try to see these for yourself if possible).

Adopt the planning format which includes options, so that you can add or leave out sections as proves appropriate. You could use an introductory exercise which gives you an idea of the learners' expectations, so that you can re-jig your plan in the opening stages of the lesson. You could do this informally with a round. In this you sit participants in a circle and ask each person to complete the sentence 'What I want from this session is . . .'.

If you feel that a structured approach would set the wrong tone, you could use the first 10 minutes to ask the students about their experiences in the topic area, such as workplace policies, incidents in their training, or items they have seen in the media. This will give you a starting point and draw the learners into the lesson. If you make opportunities for questions, and ask some of your own, you will be able to gauge the level of their understanding. Leave time at the end to ask for feedback on how they felt the lesson went, so that you can evaluate the success of your strategies.

Summary

You have now explored in detail techniques of planning which will enable you to set up long and short courses, single sessions within programmes and one-off sessions. You have seen the importance of the learning objectives in guiding your decisions about content, activities and ways of checking learning. You have seen how planning is linked in to every other stage of the teaching/training cycle.

The follow up to planning is preparation, since no design, however satisfying, will succeed without the good organisation which brings it into effect. One area of preparation which repays careful attention is that of choosing and creating teaching aids and learning resources. Let's move on to look at this next.

4 Teaching Aids and Learning Resources

Introduction

In this chapter you are going to explore the selection, production, use and evaluation of teaching aids and learning resources. You will remember that teaching aids are objects, materials and equipment used by teachers to illustrate their teaching, whereas learning resources are materials, objects or people consulted by students directly.

In the following pages you will explore the implications of using a variety of aids and resources, from both the learners' and teachers' viewpoint. We are going to focus on the capacity of the materials to stimulate learning, rather than on the technicalities of production or use. This chapter aims to rouse your imagination, to make you think freely about the many different items you can use to help your students grasp the essential messages of your teaching. You can then use specialist publications for technical guidance.

Although the chapter contains a great deal of information, it is organised around one main activity. You are going to advise a group of teachers about the most appropriate aids and resources to use in particular learning situations. In the process you will generate many ideas for your own teaching.

Meeting the case study teachers

You are now going to meet several teachers who are planning learning situations. They have researched their students' needs, clarified the lesson objectives and made tentative plans about teaching and learning strategies. Now they are reviewing the choice of aids and resources before finalising their planning.

ACTIVITY

Read through the case studies. Make some initial notes of suggestions you might make in each case. Then research your ideas in the next part of the chapter which describes the functions of a variety of aids and resources.

Wendy is to teach techniques of bandaging to a group of about 20 volunteer First Aiders, who will then be examined on this.

Andrew is working with newly appointed operating department assistants in a busy hospital. They need to become familiar with the most frequently used drugs as soon as possible.

Will knows that his brickwork students find it difficult to translate the two-dimensional drawings in their text books into three-dimensional models when they come to their practical session. He wants to make the theory easier to visualise.

Gerald is preparing health and social care students, who are all 16–17 years of age, to work with elderly patients in residential care. He wants them to understand the feelings of old people about their loss of independence.

Amin has a revision session with third-year radiographers about a week before their final theory examination. He wants to motivate the students to revise for themselves instead of relying on him to tell them everything.

Valerie is to give a talk on herbs and spices to a group of mixed cultural background and varied levels of fluency in English, in a venue with which she is unfamiliar. She can't rely on there being an overhead projector, but she needs to provide plenty of visual stimulus.

Anthony is teaching motor vehicle studies. The next topic is fuel injection systems which some students find difficult to follow, even with illustrations on the whiteboard.

You might like to devise a personal situation along the same lines as these outlines, and then look in the text which follows for solutions. You would benefit from sharing this exercise with a colleague.

Choosing aids and resources to match learning needs

First let's look for a moment at what you gain by using aids and resources. When any of us begins to learn something new we need the help of all our senses, particularly if the objects or processes are not normally visible or if we are dealing with abstract ideas. Many people on vocational courses prefer practical sessions because they get stimulus through every sense – the weight of the trowel, the smell of two chemicals mixing, the bite of just-cooked spaghetti, the sound of the car engine, the feel of different fabrics, the appeal of different colours to the eye, the sense of muscles working in harmony and so on. All of these things need to be pointed out in practical lessons so that our eyes, ears, noses, tongues and fingers can be trained to pick up important signals.

In theory sessions we need lots of second-hand stimulus to reactivate our memory of the real thing or to enable us to imagine it beforehand. When learning abstract concepts and relationships we need hooks to hang ideas on, diagrams, comparisons with familiar ideas and objects, concrete models of how abstract processes work, illustrations of every kind. It is the responsibility of those in the know, teachers, to structure and illustrate unfamiliar material so that they open the eyes of the mind for those learning. Aids and resources are a major source of illumination.

◄ **Figure 4.1**
Choosing aids and
resources.

All lessons offer opportunities for illustration, although some materials take longer
to prepare than others and some equipment may be expensive to acquire or complex
to use. You will have to weigh up a whole range of factors, even after you have
decided on the best aid or resource for the job of enhancing your students' abilities to
learn. These will include what is available to you and your skills in using it, suitable
accommodation and facilities, the cost of materials and the cost in time of organisation and preparation.

The gains in students' understanding, however, can be considerable and this will
lead to greater confidence and livelier learning. Once you have got the hang of the
basic aids you will feel more adventurous and imaginative (see Figure 4.1).

Reviewing the options

Let's now explore the uses and limitations of the range of aids and resources which
we identified earlier. If you have the opportunity, investigate some of the items mentioned below. You will find most teachers willing to share their ideas and expertise.

Using chalkboards, whiteboards and flip charts

These three items are used mainly for visual display. The **chalkboard**, black or
green, plain, with horizontal lines, graph squares or music staves, is the traditional
means of writing up information during the lesson. They are usually fixed to a wall
but may be free standing. They may roll round in a continuous scroll or be fixed.
Chalk sticks are officially dustless; you clean the board with a duster or stiff brush.

The chalkboard is most useful for simple diagrams, key points, listing student contributions to the lesson, or for leaving on display something your students may need
throughout the lesson, such as a recipe or set of instructions. A limitation is that
writing on them for any length of time is a laborious business, and takes your attention from the class. Their surfaces may be worn, which makes writing and viewing

difficult. They are not easy to see if you have impaired vision – use yellow chalk for best effect. On the other hand they do not depend on electricity.

The **whiteboard** has replaced the chalkboard in many cases, especially where chalk dust is unacceptable, as in computer rooms. It is a metallic board with a reflective white surface which can be fixed to a wall or hung from it. Some boards are free standing and double as flip chart stands. There is an expensive version which will deliver as a handout whatever is written on it; this can then be photocopied as an instant summary for the group. You write on it with dry wipe marker pens (these wipe off with a dry cloth). If you are unfortunate enough to write on them with spirit-based pens you will need methylated spirits to remove the ink. You can sometimes use the surface as a magnetic board for coloured counters, letters or outlines. The whiteboard should not be used as a substitute for an OHP screen because it reflects back the light uncomfortably. If you intend to do pre-prepared drawings on it you can cover them with a large piece of paper until they are wanted. The whiteboard can be used in the same way as the chalkboard, for key points, for student contributions, to work examples as a step-by-step guide to the class, for quick drawings and diagrams and for recording words new to the students.

The **flip chart** is a large pad of thick paper with a hole at each end at the top which allows it to be hung on a fixed or free standing frame. The individual pages can then be turned over, either for writing on or to reveal what has already been written or drawn. If you prefer, you can stick prepared material such as diagrams or photographs to the sheets, to be revealed when needed. There is also a more expensive 'post it' version of the pad which can be stuck on to surfaces without Blutak.

The pad is usefully portable. This can be very helpful if you are unfamiliar with the teaching venue and cannot rely on there being suitable boards or OHP facilities. The flip chart can also be used by students. Single sheets can be torn off to be used by small groups or syndicates for their deliberations. These can then be displayed to the full group with the aid of a little Blutak, and used as the focus of a verbal report. You can take the sheets away to analyse, and bring them back to another session if appropriate; you might, for instance, want students to compare their decision making at different stages of their learning programme.

All three items are in common use as teaching aids. They are particularly useful for short-term display, although the flip chart can be used repeatedly and is particularly useful if you want to prepare material ahead of time.

Using overhead projectors

This is a machine which projects an image above eye level on to an angled screen or a convenient white wall. You need to angle the screen forwards from the top to prevent an effect called keystoning, which is where the image on the screen is wider at the top than at the bottom. The projector stands on a special trolley or on a desk/table top and is used in normal lighting conditions. You may need to use window blinds in very bright sunshine. You stand so that you can face the class.

You produce your image either on individual acetate sheets, or on an acetate roll which can be attached to the projector so that you can write or draw on it as you talk. The sheets are called overhead transparencies, overheads or acetates. You can create your image by drawing, tracing or writing freehand, by using Letraset or by using a computer – you transfer the text or drawing on to special transparencies via a photocopier or via a computer scanner.

If you draw freehand you can choose between two kinds of special pen, one which leaves a permanent image (spirit based) or one which is water soluble and wipes off. The permanent ink can be erased with an OHP eraser if you make a mistake. The pens come in all colours and several nib thicknesses; but colours such as red, yellow and orange do not show up well.

The OHP can be both a blessing and a curse. It can provide much needed visual stimulus to enrich teacher talk or it can encourage lazy teachers to slap up sheet after sheet of notes for students to copy. As a control device for a boisterous group the latter is primitive; as an aid to learning it has no value at all. Students cannot think and write at the same time. The only use of this approach is to ask students to copy a small amount of material, after which you stop, explain, discuss, question and then continue. Some teachers like to reveal the content of an OHT step by step, by moving a covering piece of paper steadily down the image. This allows the students to respond to each point in turn. This has its uses but infuriates some students because it forces them to think along the teacher's lines rather than to think about the material for themselves. You can also lie small objects *carefully* on the OHP screen so that they are magnified, for example, different sizes of fuse.

ACTIVITY

What could **you** do with an OHP? Think of some ideas of your own before you look at the ones which follow.

Uses for the OHP

- display your objectives at the start of the session;
- generate a summary of the lesson from student contributions;
- show a cartoon to gain attention or establish a mood;
- ask small groups to record the outcomes of their discussions;
- use like a chalkboard for student contributions, to show unfamiliar words, for freehand sketches;
- display an image to help students in a practical, for example, to show a method of working or explain a complex drawing;
- link to a computer to show an enlarged image of the one on the VDU;
- build up a complex drawing, for example, of a central heating system by overlaying acetates on top of each other;
- use with an additional fitting to show movement, such as the circulation of the blood.

Good practice in the use of the OHP

You have no doubt experienced some poor practice as a learner.

ACTIVITY

Use these experiences to help you generate a set of rules which a new teacher should follow. Do this under two headings, firstly advice about the use of the machine (OHP), then advice about the design of the acetates (OHTs).

The OHP

- always check beforehand that the machine is in proper working order – and know where to go for help;
- position the machine safely, without trailing leads;
- remove the acetate and switch off the machine as soon as it is no longer needed;
- position yourself so that everyone can see clearly;
- use a pen to point to the OHP screen if you want to emphasise detail, or use a long pointer for the big screen or wall image;
- make use of the fact that you are facing the students to keep the session interactive; encourage comment and questions about the images shown.

Using overhead transparencies

- label or number your OHTs so that you don't get mixed up when using them, and store them carefully after use;
- be sparing with the amount you put on each OHT; you need only a summary or key words;
- use large clear lettering; check that it is visible from the back of the room and by all the viewers;
- use colour for interest and emphasis, but only those colours that show up well;
- use outlines rather than small detail, or use several acetates if you are showing the parts which make up a whole;
- leave a space along all the edges so that the image sits well in the middle of the screen;
- use mostly lower case lettering, which is easier to read;
- write all numbers very clearly;
- check your spelling before you produce the final image.

Using handouts and worksheets

Handout is a term used for virtually any collection of paper given out during a session to help students learn, or after it as an aid to memory and revision. As a learner you will have received many examples, some of which you will have used actively, others of which you will have filed as a kind of insurance policy. They range from closely typed or handwritten sheets of unrelieved information to cleverly designed worksheets inviting students' contributions at each stage. They are both aids and resources, often given out as a digest of the teacher's wisdom but, once in the student's grasp, a potential resource for future study and reflection. Let's review the various functions of handouts before you go on to look at good practice in their use:

- they free students to concentrate on talking, listening and thinking rather than copying;

- they promote interaction when used in small group exercises, such as completing gaps in the information, or deciding on solutions to problems;
- they allow students to individualise their work, for instance by filling in incomplete handouts;
- they can act as a record of information, a summary and a revision aid;
- they can substitute for a text if none is available.

How do **you** use handouts?

ACTIVITY

Note some ideas for using handouts in your lessons. Try to be imaginative and to promote student interaction. Here are a few examples to give you some more ideas:

Helen's handout was two sheets of paper headed respectively 'Left' and 'Right'. She was teaching foot care to female retail assistants. Their task was to draw round their own stocking feet while standing on the paper. Then they put their shoes over the drawings and drew round them. They quickly saw the point about shoe fittings. Then she gave them another handout of a drawing of the ideal shoe and asked them to indicate on it its positive features.

Effie's handout was laminated, and showed a small tortoise shape in various stages of construction. Her intention was to show her students how to model in marzipan. By following her instructions on the surface of the handout itself, they could match their marzipan to the desired shape until they achieved a completed tortoise which sat exactly over the final illustration (see Figure 4.2).

◀ **Figure 4.2**
A laminated handout can be useful.

Pryah's handout is A5 size and is designed to sit on the desk in front of each student. On it she has drawn the QWERTY keyboard her word processing students must learn to use. She is going to show them where to position their hands. Afterwards she will give them another handout of left and right hands with the letters of the home keys written on the fingers.

Robin has produced his handout using a graphics package on a computer. It shows the financial position of a large business in a series of bar charts, pie charts and graphs. His accountancy students have to summarise the information presented for the firm's annual report.

Kate has used her draftswoman's skills to draw a cross-section through one of the machines involved in producing plastic cards so that her on-the-job engineering trainees can appreciate what is going on inside the outer casing. She has given them this as a handout after going over an enlarged version of it with them on a flipchart sheet.

Good practice in the use of handouts

There are several key points to bear in mind when you use handouts.

ACTIVITY

Summarise your ideas as Ten Golden Rules, remembering to include both how you use the handout and what it looks like. You'll find some suggestions below.

Ten Golden Rules for Handouts

You should always:

1. Be certain that they will advance the lesson objectives.
2. Make sure that they are suitable for all the students, that is, they don't offend anyone and are readable by everyone.
3. Explain the point and purpose of the handout.
4. Always ask if anything needs clarifying.
5. Have enough copies.
6. Choose appropriate times and procedures for distribution.
7. Check that you are not breaking copyright.
8. Make students use them actively, in the lesson or soon afterwards; ensure absent students receive copies too.
9. Have good-quality copies.
10. Review and update them, if necessary, whenever you use them.

A collection of handouts can easily be turned into a set of learning materials for a student to use individually, maybe to catch up on an area of the course they have missed or as revision or because they prefer to learn on their own. In this case the materials need to be able to stand on their own. You will have to give very clear instructions as to how the learner is to work through them, and arrange for them to be given feedback. You might mark their work, give them an answer sheet to mark their own work or have a follow-on tutorial with them.

The simplest version of this is a **worksheet**. This usually combines some information and a task based on that information, carefully structured and at the right level of difficulty for the learner. You can base these on text book material (but check copyright with a librarian) or invent your own. Part of the task can be for students to go and look up material elsewhere, such as a library or information centre, or to interview someone or to observe a situation and learn from what they see. There is virtually no end to the possibilities. The example which follows is being used on a City & Guilds Intermediate GNVQ in Leisure and Tourism. Think how you could turn one of your handouts into this kind of interactive worksheet.

Train, Plane, Ferry or Hovercraft?

Travellers now have the option of several different forms of transport to reach their chosen destinations. At present there is great competition between tour operators aiming to take customers across the Channel to France.

Your task

You are going to cost return journeys between London and Paris for:

(a) a family of two adults and two children (7 and 13)
(b) a business woman
(c) a party of 20 young people all over 18.

You should quote in each case for:

(a) standard-class and first-class rates
(b) midweek and weekend travel
(c) high and low season.

You should consult the relevant company brochures and timetables in the practice bureau which have been put on reserve for your use until Friday. You must also ring at least one operator of each form of transport specified to enquire about this month's special offers, using the bureau telephone.

Bring your completed work to the next scheduled tutorial session.

Using textbooks

You may use textbooks so frequently and automatically that you don't think of them as a teaching aid or learning resource. Yet often the learner's first response to joining a course is to look for or ask about an appropriate accompanying book. Some students will be happy to have **a** book, others will want to have **the** book, yet others will want you to recommend a whole booklist. Some will never open it, some will dip in to it, others will read it from cover to cover. A few will go off and research books of their own to recommend to you.

A well-researched and carefully chosen text can make a world of difference to the success of your students' learning.

ACTIVITY

Think of different ways in which you could use a textbook in your subject area. If possible, compare your ideas with someone teaching a different subject from you to generate more ideas.

Why not?

- set a section for pre-reading before a lesson so that students are prepared for a discussion or task;
- turn a diagram in the book into a handout which you use in the lesson, asking them to read the rest of the text later;
- set a section for consolidation after a lesson;
- set exercises from the book for classwork or homework;
- work through sections of it with the full group;
- set sub-groups parts of it to précis and report back on;
- refer to it constantly as a reference text;
- use it as catching-up material for those who are absent;
- ask students to read aloud from it, then discuss the content;
- use it to show a different way of working from the one you have used in the session;
- use it to extend or deepen knowledge in a particular area;
- ask students to read up on parts of the syllabus you won't be covering.

Before you recommend a textbook, you need to do your own homework. Are you sure that the book:

- is relevant to the learners' objectives?
- is appropriately demanding (right level)?
- is written in language they can understand?
- is free of material which any of them might find off-putting?
- has an introduction which explains how it is to be used?
- has accurate and up-to-date information?
- follows a logical structure?

You might also want to choose a text which is reasonably portable, reasonably priced and good looking. Do make sure that there are copies in the library for those who can't afford to buy it.

Using packaged learning materials

These are materials intended to be worked on by students without the teacher present, though they may well have been introduced in a lesson or tutorial or may lead to a group or individual follow-up session. Sometimes the materials are in the form of booklets with textual material and graphics; they will probably include exercises and give feedback. They should include a clear statement of objectives. The idea is to make the learner **work** through the material, so questions are often used, as they would be in equivalent classroom sessions. A step-by-step approach is usually adopted, with material related to particular objectives and split up into manageable portions. A certain amount of guidance and encouragement is built in.

Nowadays most packages include video or audio tapes and may also include other visual materials such as charts and photographs, as with language learning materials for example. The package may be based on an interactive computer program, or may be a multimedia kit mixing computer, video and written material. You are more likely to use commercial material than to make your own, at least initially. Later you may develop your own for the sake of being able to match it closely to the learning objectives.

You may have some experience of learning in this way. If so you will know that there are both advantages and potential drawbacks. Even if you have not used packaged materials yourself, you will know from the different ways in which people learn and study that materials must be chosen with care if they are to suit the range of potential learners.

Let's look at the two sides of the argument. For those who like this approach they welcome being able to work at their own pace with exclusive use of a set of materials. They prefer not to be distracted by other learners. They respond to the step-by-step approach of many of the materials, the built-in exercises and feedback.

Critics of the approach feel that it is hard to motivate learners to start on the materials or to keep going, especially with no one else to bounce ideas off. There is the temptation to skip sections and to cheat on the exercises. Also learners need time to adjust to this style of working. Learners do indeed need considerable self-discipline to work through the materials. Recent developments in interactive video and computing have made packaged learning much more lively, but these are expensive options. You will in any case need to devise appropriate ways of monitoring the quality of the individual's engagement with the materials, and of providing support, guidance and help if difficulties are experienced. The method calls for considerable investment of tutorial time.

Using other forms of visual stimulus

There are several other ways of engaging interest and enabling learners to see the point which use less-sophisticated material. Well-chosen photographs, drawings, newspaper or magazine cuttings can be very effective, either with a group or for students working on their own. Pictures can be used to stimulate creative writing, drama or debate. Posters can create an atmosphere and convey important messages in otherwise neutral settings. Rather dreary rooms can be filled with ideas, either scene setting or technical, such as travel posters or enlarged cross-sections of machines, maps or visual dictionaries. The images can be used within the lesson for simple reference or as the focus for a class exercise.

Choose a lesson topic where you would normally only use talk and written text. Plan to use visual material to stimulate interest or to convey the point of your explanations. Ask the learners for their reactions. There is an example below.

Michèle usually asks her group of ESOL (English for Speakers of Other Languages) students to introduce themselves to each other at the beginning of the first lesson. They find this quite daunting. This time she draws the word 'welcome' in bright colours and in several different languages on pieces of cartridge paper, one piece for each language. She sticks these up round the room. Students are asked to group themselves next to their own language, greet each other in it, then prepare a sentence in it which they will pronounce and translate for the whole group. Only after that will they be asked to do the original exercise of introducing themselves in English.

Another effective way of providing visual interest is to use **slides**, either a carousel slide projector into which you first insert numbered slides in a predetermined order, or one with a hand-operated mechanism into which you insert the slides as you want them. The carousel can be operated by remote control, freeing you to interact with the viewers. You may have the facility to use two projectors, timed electronically so one slide fades into the next, with or without a taped commentary.

Slides are very useful where it is not possible to see the real thing, such as a rare skin condition or rock formation or cell structure, and for showing close-up detail. But beware of putting learners into a passive state, especially if you darken the room. You will need to work questioning and discussion into your presentation. Keep the number of slides small.

You should always warn students first if you are going to show anything which they might find distressing.

Using audio-based material

Audio material is much under-rated. Sound is a very potent stimulus, especially in vocational areas. We can conjure up whole situations from snippets of sound and gain valuable feedback about the performance of things animal, mechanical and physical. The sounds made by engines in trouble have to be learned by trainee engineers just as the nuances of a child's crying have to be recognised and interpreted by trainee midwives. Within many areas of learning sound is a crucial element; in some, such as music and languages, it is the essence of the subject. Recorded and live sound will play a large part in teaching and learning in these areas.

Recorded sound can be used in areas as diverse as teaching listening skills on a counselling course, demonstrating how the *Canterbury Tales* would have sounded when recounted by the mediaeval pilgrims, dictation for audio typists, eyewitness accounts in history lessons, or mood setting in yoga classes. It is worth thinking about ways in which you could use a cassette tape recorder to add interest and realism to your sessions. This could be as simple as recording part of a Parliamentary debate on public spending, and asking the students to continue the debate from the point it breaks off. Or you could record the sounds of car engines in trouble and get motor vehicle students to identify the causes of the problems.

Using video

Video is now so commonplace a part of everyday life that you can easily overlook its usefulness in the teaching context. Virtually any situation can be recorded from reality or in a simulation to use in the classroom, where it gives immediacy. By using short clips rather than extended sequences you can inject interest and focus attention on essential areas. Provided you observe licensing agreements (talk to the librarian or media resources manager at your place of work) you can draw from a very wide range of visual material, with the added advantages of sound and movement. In addition, students can make their own video films in the classroom or studio, or on the streets, using easily portable equipment.

ACTIVITY

Plan to use some video material in a forthcoming lesson. Afterwards evaluate your experiment with the students.

Let's look at how some other teachers did this:

Wendy is a driving instructor preparing pupils for the Advanced Driving Certificate. She has a commercial video which she lends to them close to the test date, then discusses and practises with them the points from it which they raise.

Juliana is working with a group of unemployed people who have been made redundant from management positions. They are learning to be interviewees rather than interviewers. They are simulating interview situations, which are being recorded on video so that they can analyse their performance afterwards.

Alan has set his Advanced GNVQ Art and Design students an exercise to make them look closely at familiar objects. Each has to make a 5-minute video film of a building of their choice, then use it to introduce the building to the group, explaining why they found its construction or decoration interesting.

What is it about the ways these teachers are using video which turns it into a learning aid rather than just entertainment?

- they are using the material to solve a particular problem, such as to arouse interest, to create interaction, or to give feedback;
- they have clear objectives for the sessions;
- they have chosen appropriate timing in the learning sequence;
- they use short sequences or clips rather than long programmes;
- the students have to be actively involved with the video, during or immediately after seeing it;
- the learning required could not be conveyed without the visual stimulus.

Using three-dimensional models

You can buy ready-made models from educational suppliers of, for example, atomic structures, life-size skeletons, or cut-away models of the heart. You can take your students to visit local natural history or science museums which often have splendid working models, such as the inside of a hive, railway or automobile engines, or weather formations. Some museums have models of domestic interiors, others of agricultural and industrial processes. Some even simulate historical experiences, such as being in an air raid shelter during World War II. They may be able to convey aspects of the experience which even CD ROM cannot, such as characteristic smells in engineering or the smallness of the space in a submarine. Or you can make your own models from spare parts or everyday materials, such as a circuit board to demonstrate wiring.

What do you think you will gain from going to all this trouble? Models of the whole or parts of an object can enable you to:

- show a structure in simplified form;
- show something normally invisible to the naked eye;
- make abstract ideas concrete;
- show the stages of a process step by step;
- be larger than life to reveal obscure features;
- involve the students actively, for example in handling the model.

Using computers

Advances in computer technology over the last few years have opened up all manner of learning opportunities both in places of learning (see Figure 4.3) and in the home. You can use the computer itself as a teacher, both as an information bank of almost infinite resource and/or as a tutor. The degree of interactiveness is increasing steadily, as is the ease of access to the computer's different functions. You can set up the excitement of discovery learning within a structured framework which leads to the fulfilment of specific learning objectives. The advent of multimedia means that not only do systems have greater visual appeal, but you could, if you wished, author your own material for particular groups of learners. On a simpler level the greater availability of word processing facilities allows you to produce more professional looking handout material. This can be taken a stage further if you have access to a desk top publishing system.

If you are unfamiliar with computer technology you could talk to the learning resources staff in your place of work to see what the possibilities are for your students. Perhaps they could:

- use CD ROM to find information for projects and assignments, such as newspaper items, entries in encyclopaedias, maps of the world, or collections of statistics;
- follow a self-teach programme on how to create spreadsheets so they can handle numerical data;
- create databases of information, such as mailing lists, that they will need regularly in their studies;
- forecast future patterns, for example, of population growth, weather conditions, economic growth rates, or comparative health standards;
- produce their assignments as word processed documents;
- use a graphics package to design such things as fashion garments, body parts for cars, household furniture, logos and so on;
- use numeracy programmes to extend their application of number;

◄ **Figure 4.3**
Accessing information
through the computer is
now common practice.

- work through a decision-making programme in which they role-play people in key occupational positions, such as care professionals, traffic controllers, security officers, accountants and so on;
- learn to identify classes and categories of items, for instance, biological specimens, cloud formations, types of brickwork bonds, mathematical symbols, bird calls, cell structures and so on.

As you can see, there are many possibilities. Some of them are faster and livelier versions of what students have always done in libraries and, as such, likely to motivate reluctant readers. You should also investigate computer-assisted learning for any of your students with learning difficulties, and special adaptations for learners with impaired sight or dexterity. Again, ask your colleagues or contact the responsible bodies, like the RNIB, for help.

Using everyday objects

If you are able to bring into your lesson examples of 'the real thing' this will have considerable impact. You do this all the time in practical sessions, of course, working directly with the materials or equipment concerned, as in carpentry, food preparation or hairdressing. During demonstration you show examples of products at different stages of preparation and in their final state so that students can match their performance to yours. It is in theory sessions that learners need most help. The operation of the carburettor can be much more readily appreciated if key pieces of machinery can be examined alongside OHT images and your description.

Don't assume that the real thing will be familiar to your learners, especially if they are in the younger age groups. Check assumptions such as that all the students in an accountancy class will own and use a cheque book, that GNVQ Hospitality and

Catering students will have eaten from silver service or stayed in a hotel, that Leisure and Tourism students will have travelled on aircraft or been abroad, or that students of English literature will have seen a play in a theatre. You may have to provide lots of second-hand experiences through practical activities and simulations.

Using people

People are also learning resources. You may be able to arrange for people with particular life or work experience to visit your students, who can then interview them about matters relevant to their objectives. This is a beneficial process in its own right in developing communication skills. You may not have to look far for experts, other students often prove to have knowledge and expertise that you could use, as do staff in other parts of your organisation. Then there are parents, friends and business contacts, local employers, speakers from a wide range of voluntary bodies and representatives of the public services. Most will be pleased to be invited and will not require payment. The only constraint may prove to be your imagination.

You have now reviewed a wide range of teaching aids and learning resources which will help you to:

- create interest and motivation;
- develop understanding of concepts, processes and relationships;
- involve students actively in their learning.

Begin where you feel most comfortable and develop your skills gradually, basing your use of resources on approaches which will help your students learn, rather than those which will make life easier for yourself in the short term.

Advising on the use of aids and resources

Let's now return to the group of teachers whom you have been preparing to advise on their use of teaching aids and learning resources for specified sessions. You will have lots of ideas to propose. Compare your solutions with the ones which follow.

Wendy, teaching techniques of bandaging to volunteer First Aiders, could:

- run through the routine step by step on the OHP;
- demonstrate using a student 'victim';
- display enlarged drawings of each stage of the process on flip chart pages;
- refer them to the chapter in their *Manual of First Aid*;
- bandage up volunteers representing each stage of the process so each acts as a live aid;
- consolidate key points on a handout.

Andrew, teaching anaesthetic practices, could:

- devise case studies requiring particular drugs which they research and report on;
- show a manufacturer's video;
- set up a discovery session where they use manufacturers' packaging and leaflets to research the information, which he then summarises on a flip chart, OHT or whiteboard.

Will, teaching brickwork, could:

- use a graphics package on a computer, linked to a device on the OHP, to show how objects look when rotated;
- make models out of small-scale bricks for students to handle;
- draw both 2-D and 3-D outlines of the same object on OHT or handout so that students can work to a guide.

Gerald, wanting to help young Health and Social Care students to understand the feelings of elderly people about loss of independence, could:

- make and play a tape of personal accounts by old people, real or simulated, to stimulate discussion;
- get the students to interview elderly people they know, and report back to the class;
- arrange a visit to a residential home where students talk to residents, and discuss this afterwards;
- set up a role play about elderly people talking to each other or care professionals about their feelings;
- use a series of case studies which he invents.

Amin, wanting to encourage radiography students to do their own revision, could:

- devise a self-test worksheet or workbook for each to complete;
- show slides of certain conditions whose treatment students must research;
- set up a competitive situation in the form of a game modelled on a well-known version, such as *University Challenge* – students revise beforehand so that their team will win;
- allocate parts of the syllabus to pairs of students who have to revise and then teach the others key points.

Valerie needs to illustrate a talk on herbs and spices for a group of mixed language and culture. She could:

- use pictures cut from cookery and gardening magazines, linking the plant to its culinary uses;
- laminate the pictures for handing round;
- prepare the pages of a flip chart pad with drawings which she can reveal in ordered sequence – she could leave space to add plant names in other languages which the students tell her;
- prepare a handout, which is the small-scale version of the flip chart, for consolidation and later reference;
- take in fresh and dried herb and plant samples, in clear plastic envelopes which can be opened to reveal their smell.

Anthony, teaching about fuel injection systems, could:

- do a series of free-hand drawings on the whiteboard;
- bring in the parts and show how they interact;
- play extracts from a manufacturer's video;
- use the OHP to show parts and movement;
- demonstrate on a stripped-down car in the workshop.

Evaluating your use of aids and resources

Finally we come to the matter of your evaluation of your effectiveness in using aids and resources.

There are a number of questions you will want to ask yourself. They will probably include:

- were the materials relevant to the learning objectives?
- did the resources improve students' learning?
- did the choice of aids disadvantage anyone?
- was the cost in time, money and effort justified?

You will be able to use your own judgement to some degree to answer these questions, but the learners' views are also very relevant. You might like to devise a regular routine whereby you invite your students to comment on the materials you use, perhaps as part of a wider evaluation of your lessons. You could also arrange to share your intentions and findings with a colleague, and discuss any changes you both feel are desirable.

Here is an example of a check sheet for your students.

Evaluation Sheet: Aids and Resources

I would like you to tell me whether the aids/resources I have used in this session have helped you to learn. Please give me some feedback to the questions below. This will help me to improve my teaching and your learning. Thank you.

1. Did I explain to you clearly how I or you would use the aid/resource? How could I have done this better?
2. Did you have enough time to use the material? How could this have been better?
3. Were you able to use the aid/resource comfortably? How could this have been improved?
4. Did you feel at ease with the content of the aid/resource? How could this have been improved?
5. How did the aid/resource help you to learn? Please give at least one example.
6. Have you any suggestions for other aids/resources you or I could use to deal with this subject?

Summary

Now that you have explored the potential for using a wide variety of aids and resources, from simple handouts to computer programs, you will be in a position to choose the most appropriate materials for your own students. You will bear in mind, in all cases:

- the relevance of the material to the learning objectives;
- the suitability of the material to the group/individuals;
- practical considerations of cost, availability and training.

It is important to take advantage of the many possibilities for aiding learning, even if you have only ever used handouts. You will find plenty of people willing to help you develop your ideas. You could start by taking a stock check of your own knowledge and abilities.

ACTIVITY

Make yourself an action plan for developing your expertise, beginning with those items which are of most obvious value to your students, and which are available where you work.

You will find the material you have looked at here very relevant to the next chapter, *Presenting Information and Ideas*.

5 Presenting Information and Ideas

This chapter is about the teacher's or trainer's role in organising and communicating information and ideas to learners. This is a formal activity, variously called giving presentations, lecturing, teacher talk or exposition. The essential teacher activities are telling and explaining, and inviting and answering questions. You may use visual aids, or you may suggest that students take notes while you talk. You may ask students from time to time to carry out such activities as completion of a gapped handout, discussion in a small group or completion of an exercise in a textbook. Although the material is for the students' benefit, you are the dominant figure and in control of the interaction.

In this chapter you will explore the uses of presentation methods, their advantages and disadvantages, techniques for their organisation and the communication skills you will need to use the methods effectively. The most important part of the chapter is the discussion of your communication skills and responsibilities, particularly in explaining and questioning.

This chapter is closely related to several others, in particular the one which follows, *Organising Learning in Groups*, which shows how you can consolidate learning from presentations by the use of exercises in small groups.

You could also look back at Chapter 3 *Planning for Learning* and Chapter 4 *Teaching Aids and Learning Resources* to consider how you would choose and structure your material for a period of exposition, and how you might use teaching aids to enhance your delivery and the students' learning. There is also helpful material in Chapter 7 *Teaching a Skill* on communicating effectively when giving information through demonstration.

Uses of presentation methods

There are several reasons why you might choose a period of explanation and related questioning as one of the strategies from which your students might learn. The simplest is that you want to give them information. This might be about an event, such as the passing of an Act of Parliament, or a process, such as the way parliamentary candidates are selected. You could describe scientific experiments, local government procedures, health care regimes, life histories, economic theories – the list is endless.

Decide how **you** could use a 20-minute period of explaining and questioning at the beginning of one of your own sessions. Then look at some ideas from Monica, who runs short courses in information technology. Monica could:

- introduce a new topic, such as spreadsheets;
- explain new jargon terms which will come up in the session;
- recap material from previous sessions;
- explain a crucial principle, such as input–output relationships;
- describe business applications of an IT process, such as a database;
- outline a case study which the students will then work on;
- describe health and safety issues in working with VDUs.

As you can see there are several possibilities just in the opening period of a session. You might also want to develop a theory, show how a principle can be applied in practice, stimulate ideas on a problem, explain interrelationships or narrate a series of events.

Advantages of presentation methods

The main advantage of the method is its usefulness for several purposes, as you have just seen. It also has a number of practical advantages. These include:

- teacher talk needs very few resources in connection with equipment, specialist accommodation or aids;
- students are familiar with the approach and don't need preparation or training;
- you are in control of the timing of the session;
- you are unlikely to disrupt any other set of people with, for example, noise;
- you can take the place of a text book, film or video if these are unavailable.

More importantly, the opportunity to talk to the group can enable you to mould the way they think about a subject or activity. You can encourage a positive approach to the topic, such as towards safe practices in the workshop, or to study techniques. You can stimulate their desire to learn through your own enthusiasm for the material. You can make it real by your choice of example, analogy or anecdote. You can make it credible by relating it to work practice.

And you can make it **comprehensible** by choosing the right level and pace for their understanding, by building new material on the foundations of what is already known and by structuring the information and ideas logically. Most helpful of all, you can give your students an overview which shows them how the parts of the subject relate to the whole, so that they have a map of the route and a sense of direction. In other words, the control which presentation methods gives you is not just control of who does what, but a much more positive control of how learners can approach and think within the subject.

Imagine, for example, how easily you could induce a negative attitude in a training session about dealing with the public, if you presented material in a cynical or flippant way. Or how you could make students apprehensive about a new topic if you presented it as being difficult. Or how you could confuse your group if you launched into an advanced topic without reference to earlier stages of learning.

When it is handled responsibly, a period of exposition within a teaching/training session is a marvellous learning resource.

Limitations of presentation methods

The main limitation of the teacher talk approach is that the learners are relatively passive. It is fatally easy to do all their thinking for them – and then to be cross that they have not learned to think things out for themselves. No amount of talk, however well structured or full of examples, will enable students to learn **unless** they are made to use or apply the material quite soon after the exposition: in fact, the sooner the better, the best time being within the session itself. You can do this by using questions, buzz groups, exercises from books or handouts, and practical activities.

Inexperienced teachers often describe their role as 'standing up in front of a class talking', about which they are understandably nervous, fearing particularly that they will dry up. This is to confuse teaching with after-dinner speaking or the specialist lecture of a visiting expert. There is a place for the well-constructed witty exposition with its anecdotes, but it is seldom the classroom.

There are two issues here. It is unrealistic to expect the teacher/trainer to be the source of all information, interpretation and stimulus. We tend to forget that information and interpretation can easily be obtained from other sources, particularly via information technology. Part of your talk time might be better spent directing learners to sources of up-to-date material and showing them how to retrieve it, study skills which they would then have for life.

Secondly, very few of us can listen actively for more than 15–20 minutes at a time, and for only a little longer than this when visual materials are used as a stimulus. Researchers have shown that we have a pattern of concentration followed by attention lapses (Figure 5.1). We do best at the beginning and end of periods of continuous listening, but we soon forget even this material unless we put it to use.

Taking notes during lectures does not help much either, apart from keeping us awake, as it is not possible to receive, think about and note material all at the same time. At best we are taking out an insurance policy on material to learn up later. The business of taking down endless notes from the OHP is about controlling the group, not about promoting high-quality learning.

◀ **Figure 5.1**
Listening is hard work.

What learners need is a short burst of material focusing on key points, followed by a period of questioning and an exercise or activity to drive home, that is, consolidate, the message. A 1-hour session would work better looking like this

> 5-min recap of previous session
> 10-min explanation of key point
> 5-min questioning for understanding
> 10-min talk on related points
> 5-min question-and-answering session
> 10-min short activity, such as buzz group
> 5-min checking of responses
> 5-min summary
> 5-min signposting of next session

than like this

> 5-min recap of previous session
> 40-min talk with OHTs for notetaking
> 5-min question-and-answer session
> 5-min direction of follow-up study
> 5-min signposting of next session

Getting organised

Let's now explore the factors which lead to effective learning from presentation methods.

ACTIVITY

Think back to sessions where you were being talked or lectured at. Can you recall aspects which made it difficult for you to gain full value from the occasions? The list which follows is a catalogue of disasters, but all of these things can happen.

A poor presentation session

- room stuffy, poor ventilation, too small for size of group;
- hard chairs;
- speaker went far too fast;
- a lot of this went over my head;
- speaker didn't check what we already knew;
- monotonous voice, I lost interest;
- used jargon without explanation;
- why are senior managers always described as 'he'?;
- hardly ever looked at my side of the room;
- used lots of clichés and kept saying 'OK';
- couldn't see visual aids, writing too small, colours faint;
- gave us a 10-page handout, I needn't have come;
- seemed to be all over the place, no structure.

> There are lots of sins in this account, not least the unsatisfactory environment and the poor communication style. The main faults are to do with lack of planning and organisation, particularly a failure to suit the way the material was selected and structured to the needs of the particular learning group.

Learners have four main requirements from exposition sessions:

- that the content is relevant to their present needs;
- that the material is at a level they can understand;
- that the material is organised logically so that they can follow it;
- that they have an opportunity to clarify points and ask questions.

If you can meet these requirements you will have gone a very long way to providing effective learning opportunities for your particular students.

ACTIVITY

Now make a checklist for an effective presentation/lecture/talk based on the four areas itemised above. If you were to set this out as a chart, you could use it to check how well you performed the next time you are responsible for such a session.

Criteria for an effective presentation/lecture/talk

(that is, relevance, level, structure, questioning)

Did I?

- relate material to the session and course objectives;
- relate material to the students' occupational or social concerns;
- provide accurate and up-to-date information and ideas;
- take into account students' previous learning and present abilities;
- explain any new terms introduced;
- use examples within/from students' experience;
- use simple ideas to introduce more complex ones;
- relate abstract ideas to concrete examples;
- tell them how the talk would be structured;
- have an introduction and a summary;
- follow a logical sequence of ideas;
- emphasise the key points to be remembered;
- invite questions at intervals and at the end;
- ask questions at intervals to check understanding.

Organising yourself – the material

Jane, a hospital dietician, is due to give a lecture to ward staff about diet and eating regimes for patients suffering from motor neurone disease. She knows that their main need is for accurate information drawn from recent research. She has checked a number of specialist journals and has a handout for them of references to articles in the hospital library and elsewhere. She has also contacted the head office of the

Motor Neurone Association who have briefed her on their own recommendations to carers.

Brian has spent the morning in the local university library going through recent law cases on road traffic accidents (RTAs) for his session with A-level law students in the sixth form college where he works. He has called up references in Law Society reports and in the press which he intends to quote. He will pass on the references to the students.

Both teachers have made sure that the information needs of their students can be met. Perhaps it is appropriate for you to follow the same kind of procedure, or maybe your checks on current data and practice involve talking to colleagues, visiting a modern business office or ringing some contacts in the trade. As a result you will now feel confident to give information, interpret material and handle any queries.

Organising yourself – the learners

You will remember that in Chapter 3 *Planning for Learning* you explored in detail the need to identify and understand your students' aims, goals, learning styles and current abilities. You used your insights to plan their learning routes and your own teaching or training sessions. Look back at the chapter to recap the 'homework' you need to do now.

Organising yourself – the environment

Much of the success of any session comes from thorough preparation. It is always worth giving attention to the learning environment. Some aspects of it may be out of your control, but if you can, make decisions about:

- the seating arrangements;
- where you position yourself and your notes, if needed;
- where you position equipment, for example OHP or computer.

Learners who are sitting in a relatively passive state for a period of time will be more affected by discomfort or distraction than those who are active. So take time to check ventilation, level of light and heating. Remember that if you have students with visual or hearing difficulties you will need to check the clarity of any visual material, and your own audibility – you could stand close by, and face anyone who needs to lip read.

Health, safety and welfare

If you have checked the points above you will have cared for the comfort of your learners. Their safety is also your responsibility. This applies just as much in a session which is devoted to knowledge and understanding as it does to a practical session. If you are using an unfamiliar room you will need to check on fire and evacuation procedures; and tell the students at the start of the session, when you register or note their names. If you are using electrical or electronic aids you will need to check that they are working properly and are not in an unsafe condition. Remember to position the OHP without trailing leads.

You should also check the state of chairs and tables and put out of bounds any that threaten collapse. If you have a flickering strip light, report it for everyone's sake, but particularly for anyone susceptible to epileptic or migraine attacks. Finally, be sure you know the accident report procedures and where to get help in an emergency.

Communicating effectively when using presentation methods

What kind of experience do most of us want as listeners and learners? Assuming that the information we are receiving is relevant to our needs and at the right level for our understanding, what are we looking for in the communication skills of the speaker?

ACTIVITY

Decide on five or six aspects which you would require.
  Here are some suggestions:

- audibility;
- clarity of diction;
- a comfortable pace for listening;
- lively speech rhythms;
- appropriate accompanying gestures;
- sufficient eye contact to make learners feel included;
- active listening style in response to questions;
- non-discriminatory language (gender, ethnicity, age, and so on);
- absence of distracting vocal mannerisms, such as throat clearing;
- absence of distracting physical mannerisms, such as pacing about.

Your communication style – explaining

As you build up a relationship with your groups of learners they will give you some feedback on your style of communication. But it is better to be brave and monitor yourself. You could arrange to audio or video tape some of your teaching, preferably with different types of group so that you can see if you vary your style significantly, for example, between younger and older students. You could ask a trusted friend to sit in on a session to give you factual information, such as how often you say 'OK', the pace of your delivery and so on.

Why not make a checklist which you can use for self-evaluation or your friend could use for observation and recording?

ACTIVITY

Draw up a possible set of questions to which you would like feedback. Then look at the example below which was created by Toni, teaching Social Policy to GNVQ Advanced Health and Social Care students.

Communication style checklist

Do I?

- Speak clearly so that all my words can be heard;
- Go at a comfortable pace for listeners (including those whose first language is not English);
- Have an accent which obscures some words;
- Use dialect or eccentric words;
- Use colloquial language inappropriately;
- Use words or phrases which some of my students might find offensive;
- Explain all jargon, and write up newly introduced and foreign words;
- Use irritating phrases, such as OK, you know what I mean, obviously;
- Explain a point in different ways if someone finds my first explanation difficult;
- Make it clear when I am asking a question which needs an answer;
- Sound interested in what I am saying;
- Look at students often, but not so intently as to make them feel uncomfortable;
- Include all parts of the room when I am talking;
- Look inviting when I ask for questions.

You will develop your own style as your confidence grows, but it is useful to monitor from the outset to guard against any barriers that you may be setting up, and to practise techniques which you can see are helpful to your students. You may find that you have one main habit which you want to work on. If so, you could write a message to yourself which you look at from time to time while talking. Some common examples are:

> *Slow down   Smile   Shut up   Ask for questions   Wait for an answer   Look all round the room   Give an example   Speak more quietly   Come out from behind the desk   Check the time*

You have now examined aspects of your style when communicating with a group of learners during a presentation or talk. The main activities you are engaged in are telling, explaining and questioning. We have dealt mainly with telling and explaining so far. Let's now look at one of the most subtle and crucial teacher skills – questioning.

Your communication style – questioning

The greatest value for the learner in being in a live session, rather than reading a book or using a computer program, is to ask and answer questions and to listen to other learners' questions and answers.

Inviting questions from the group

Inexperienced teachers are often nervous about asking for questions from the group; they 'forget' to ask, or leave it to the last moment to avoid any response. Understandably you may fear that you won't know the answer, or that there may not be any questions and there will be an awkward silence. Other worries are that you won't understand what the questioner is asking, or that you won't understand the speaker's accent, and be embarrassed in front of the class. It is also possible that one of the learners may take over the session by jumping in continuously with questions.

These are all situations which you will soon cope with after a little experience. Shy learners can be put in pairs to consult and come up with questions. You can look up something you don't know and tell them at the next meeting. You can ask people to rephrase their questions or even write them down. The value of inviting questions is that you grasp very quickly those areas of learning about which students feel uncertain, or where they have a point to make, or where there is further interest and motivation. Its greatest value is in pointing out to you where your explanations have not been sufficiently clear or detailed, or where you have failed to give examples to illustrate your points. Let's look at when and how in your session you could go about inviting questions.

When to invite questions

You will need to decide what is best for you, given the topic and the outcomes of the session, but there is plenty of scope.

ACTIVITY

Suggest appropriate times to invite questions within a lecture/talk session.
   Here are some ideas:

(1) At the beginning; this enables you to find out what learners already know and what they want to find out. They then listen actively to your presentation to look for their answers.
(2) After the first section of your talk; this enables you to discover if you and the group have a common understanding, and to clear up any early misconceptions before they develop.
(3) After each main section; this focuses attention on each portion of the material in turn and encourages questioners to be specific. It clears up difficulties while they are fresh in the memory.
(4) At the end; this is an opportunity for general questions, niggling worries or interest in further learning to be expressed.

How to ask for questions

The golden rule is never to ask 'Any questions?', because you won't get any. The request is altogether too general and unfocused. It also slightly suggests that questions would be the exception. We are all familiar with teachers who say this, having run out of time, while gathering their papers together or looking in horror at their watches. Their body language says very clearly, 'Don't ask'.

The solution is to imply that you are expecting several questions, for example

   'Now, let's have your questions, please raise your hand so that I don't miss anybody'

If there is no immediate response you could divide up the room or the topic as a prompt, for example

'Anyone in the front row, left-hand side, group over here?'

or

'We've been looking at people on site, any questions about the sequence of working or who reports to whom?'

If there is still no response, and you have 10 minutes in hand, put people into pairs to buzz for 3 minutes during which time they must come up with at least one question on something they are still not clear about. You then have 2 minutes to collect the questions and 5 minutes to answer some of them.

The way you speak is only part of the story; you need to look interested and willing to answer. The way in which you deal with the first few questions will dictate what happens thereafter. If you give a straightforward reply, either reinforcing earlier statements or adding further information, you will encourage other students to ask their questions.

Always check after giving your answer that the enquirer is indeed answered to their satisfaction – you may not have understood their question. Patience demonstrated at this stage will save crossed wires later, as well as helping the class to feel safe with you and respect you. If you can involve others in the group in elaborating the answer this will add to the interaction.

If a question is really out of order, or needs a lengthier answer than you have time for, or will disturb the flow of the material, then arrange to speak to the questioner at the end of the session. Remember that you are 'in charge'; as long as you respond positively, you are at liberty to tell a questioner that you are about to explain their point, or would like to refer it to a little later in the session where it will fit in better for the whole class.

Putting questions to the learners

Asking questions gives you the feedback you need about the learners' level of understanding. It is very important to include questioning in lectures or talks because presentation methods give you very little of this kind of feedback. You can ask questions at several stages in a session, to achieve various purposes.

ACTIVITY

Make a chart of when and why you might question your students in one of your sessions. Afterwards, consider the following suggestions.

When to ask	Reason for asking
At the beginning	To check previous learning and current understanding To get people thinking about the subject

When to ask	Reason for asking
After each section of the material	To make them use material straight away To create an expectation of questioning throughout the session
After a key point	To confirm a grasp of basics To emphasise its importance
Whenever attention drops	To remotivate students
At the end	To underline main points To clarify misunderstanding

In other words, questions can be asked at any point in the lesson, if they are justified. But think carefully about the type of questions you put to the class generally, and those which you create for particular people whom you perceive to have a particular need. Inventing and targeting questions is a highly skilled activity which repays a lot of preparation and practice.

How to ask questions

Let's look briefly now at the tactics to adopt for asking questions within teacher talk/lecture sessions. You will find some more ideas about questioning during instruction and demonstration in Chapter 7 *Teaching a Skill*.

First think about your student group; are they robust youngsters lately from school, business people on an intensive short course, adult returners in an unfamiliar environment and so on? There are no golden rules about style. There are teachers who stick to the old formula (perfected in the armed forces) of 'pose, pause and pounce'. There are others who say you should never ask individuals by name, and yet others who say all questions should be angled towards individuals in relation to their degree of understanding. It is certainly wise to be aware of the sensitivities within your own group, including of people who have been educated in a different country, whose expectations of appropriate classroom behaviour could be quite different from yours.

There are two aspects of questioning which may be confused; one concerns the way you structure questions to **encourage learning**. The other concerns how you target and pose questions to **encourage learners**.

Questioning to encourage learning

You need to ask **open questions**. These have answers other than 'yes' or 'no', and make learners think, explain, justify, analyse or evaluate. Most of these questions will begin with **'Why?'** and **'How?'** rather than **'What?'**, **'When?'**, **'Who?'**. For example

'Why do you need to know the temperature in different parts of your refrigerator?'

'How would you introduce appraisal to a firm you had just joined as managing director?'

Questions to encourage learners

If you want to motivate and engage learners, then you need to ask questions in ways that are not perceived as a threat. This is why you need to know your own students **and** understand how adults learn and how they feel about themselves as learners. **Your main responsibility is to preserve learners' self-esteem**. How can you do this?

ACTIVITY

Think back to moments in your own learning when you were made to feel uncomfortable, and those when you were put at ease, when questions were being asked. What advice can you give?
   Here are some suggestions:

- ask a question clearly in the session which is well within the learners' capacity, to give them confidence;
- ask everyone to write down an answer and to check it with a neighbour before offering it to you;
- ask diffident people supplementary questions after bolder students have answered the main question.

Responding to the answers you are given

Almost as important as the way you ask the question is the way you deal with the answer. Think of three phrases you would **never** want a teacher to use to you. They might include:

'Hmmmmmmm' (while looking away)
'Good lord'
'Don't be stupid'
'Were you listening?'
'There's always someone makes that mistake'
'I should have known better than ask you'

Learners are most likely to be encouraged to answer if you listen carefully to their points, don't jump in before they have finished speaking, and confirm the acceptability of their answer. Even if 'No' is required it can be tempered with phrases which encourage another attempt, like 'Close' or 'Try again'. Try to convey credit for attempting an answer, even if the content is not ideal.

Not everyone agrees with giving praise for answers they feel the students should have known, though they will acknowledge exceptional responses. Maybe a balance is required between over-enthusiasm, which can seem insincere, and a mean little nod. It is better to be flexible than to have hard and fast rules.

Using aids with presentation methods

This topic is explored thoroughly in Chapter 4 *Teaching Aids and Learning Resources*, so only a few main points are mentioned here.

The great advantage of teaching aids to sessions of teacher talk is that they **illustrate** your meaning. A simple whiteboard or flip chart sheet can help you in some circumstances as much as a video clip or computer demonstration. The overhead projector will allow you to make your key points with text, diagrams, drawings, cartoons, silhouettes and movement.

However, you need to bear in mind two points. The first is that presentation methods tend to put learners in a passive role. This can be strongly reinforced if aids are used too often or for too long at a time, or if they are items associated with entertainment and relaxation, such as video or slides. Students can also become mesmerised by the bright light and hum of the OHP. They may lose rather than focus their concentration.

Secondly, aids inexpertly used, or which break down, can distract and irritate learners because they hold you responsible for the smooth flow of the exposition. You will need to have checked your own skills and the equipment.

The aid which can be most flexible, helpful but also damaging to a period of teacher talk is the handout. Many lectures have been ruined by the clumsy distribution of an excessive number of handouts. Even worse is to tell learners at the **end** of the session that you have a handout covering all the material which they have just struggled to get down. And, if it covers **all** of it, did they need to attend at all? On the other hand, a carefully composed handout could form a useful summary of the key points of the session, and be a revision aid; especially if it is the incomplete variety which the students complete as part of the session.

You could now read, or reread, Chapter 4 *Teaching Aids and Learning Resources*, planning how you might use them within your periods of presentation.

Consolidating learning from presentation sessions

As you saw earlier, the best way to help students to use what they hear during lectures or periods of teacher talk is to organise follow-up activities. These can be simple question and answer sessions, a test, a class exercise alone or in a small group, or a later task or assignment in which they use the information and ideas. In this way they 'fix' your material from the session and make it part of their own learning.

The next chapter, *Organising Learning in Groups*, will show you how you can choose, invent and organise this kind of consolidation activity.

Summary

In this chapter you have investigated the use of periods of teacher talk (also called lectures, exposition or presentations). You have explored their functions and their advantages and limitations. You have seen how important it is to vary the stimulus in order to keep learners actively engaged. You thought about the use of questioning to provide this stimulus and to check on students' understanding. You also analysed aspects of your communication style, both when you are presenting information and ideas and when you are dealing with questions. You saw that both your words and your body language were important elements in promoting students' learning.

The next chapter, *Organising Learning in Groups*, moves forward from this point to show you how you can set up exercises and activities to involve learners actively in consolidating their learning.

6 Organising Learning in Groups

Learning with groups of other learners is an option favoured by many students because it gives them both stimulus and support. They enjoy the opportunity to share ideas and experiences, and appreciate the range of different perspectives they gain from group activities. They also value the supportive learning environment initiated by the teacher and maintained by group members for their mutual benefit. For many people, joining a learning group is preferable to individual tuition or interacting with learning resources. In fact, on many courses, they are able to experience something of all three approaches.

This chapter is about exercises and activities which you can set up for groups of learners, both in the full group and in sub-groups of it which you create for particular purposes. These activities can be seen as valuable learning situations in their own right, or as a complement to learning gained from presentation methods. 'Typical' teaching sessions often consist of a period of formal exposition followed by an exercise for the whole group or a small task to be done in sub-groups. The full group is then brought back together for feedback and a summary of the learning achieved. You are going to investigate the range of suitable activities for full and sub-group use. In the process you will examine your responsibilities and the skills you will need to develop as organiser and leader.

The benefits of learning through group activities

On a practical level, group work changes the role of the student from relatively passive to active. There is an expectation that all members of the large or small group will be involved. You may give them roles such as sub-group leader, scribe and reporter. Their peers pressure them to contribute ideas to group tasks. They are expected to produce findings which they write up on flip chart paper or OHP acetates, or stand up and tell the rest of the class.

From your point of view all this activity increases students' motivation, encourages them to feel responsible for their learning, shows you evidence of that learning, and is generally fun.

From the students' point of view it is a more adult way of learning, with degrees of consultation and negotiation, where their own life and work experience are seen as valuable contributions to the group's achievements. It helps to equalise the gap between their own and the teacher's expertise.

Another benefit is that students can be made more aware of the learning process itself, rather than taking everything for granted. This shows up in their greater ability to evaluate their courses and lessons.

In cognitive terms, group activities are effective in developing higher-order thinking skills, taking students beyond memorisation into application, analysis and evaluation. For instance they can be encouraged to:

- analyse complex situations;
- apply principles to concrete situations;
- generate new ideas;
- develop solutions to problems;
- evaluate solutions against criteria.

Within the group, especially in sub-groups, students whom you have thought quite weak in thinking skills may well improve markedly under such concentrated peer-led activity.

The other great advantage of group work in learning terms is that it contributes to the development of interpersonal skills and attitudes. Students learn to listen to and consider views other than their own. They learn to interact with a range of people in a structured way (Figure 6.1). They have to research other people's situations and feelings, to put themselves into their shoes. Both the content and the process of group work can spur considerable development in individual learners.

In the material which follows you will read about organising and managing activities in both full group and sub-groups. As each kind of activity is described, you might like to think about how you could use it within your own teaching or training.

ACTIVITY

Draw up a chart, similar to that shown in Figure 6.2, which you add to as you work through the chapter, using the headings given there. Discuss your ideas with a colleague if possible. Then draw up an action plan to set up the activities or to develop the skills you think you will need.

◀ Figure 6.1
Students contribute ideas and experiences.

Chosen activity	Student objectives	My role
For example,		
Case study	Interaction in class Listening to others Problem solving	Writing the study Briefing students Managing the group

◀ Figure 6.2
Advantages of group learning activities.

Organising learning activities for the full group

In this chapter the term 'full group' can mean any number between about 8 and about 20, although you could carry out most of the activities with up to 24 people. The phrase implies that all the group are learning together, probably in the same room at the same time, for most of the activity. They may be divided into smaller groups for planning activities, such as for preparing a role play, but essentially they are all working together. Later in the chapter you can compare this kind of inter-action with a situation where the main group is split into sub-groups for most of the time, and are only together at the beginning and end of the period.

All the activities described in this chapter are *structured*. You may hear discussion or role play described as 'informal methods'. This is not an accurate description. They may seem informal compared with students sitting quietly in rows being lec-tured, but each activity has been carefully planned by the teacher, students are briefed and debriefed, they have definite roles and the activities follow a set routine. The teacher or trainer will have done a lot of the work **before** the session, so may appear less active than usual. You will soon see that they are indeed in control and very active, but in a less obvious way than might be expected. This is one of their skills.

Let's now go through the activities you could employ when working with full groups.

Brainstorming

This is an activity where one person, who may be the teacher, invites ideas from the whole group on a topic or problem. The ideas are called out by group members and written up on a board or chart by the leader. No ideas are rejected and none are com-mented on at this stage. The purpose of this is to encourage the free flow of ideas and to value them equally. No one looks foolish, everyone participates, but without pres-sure.

Once the board is full, the group then sifts the ideas for those which have potential for solving the stated problem. The leader may categorise the ideas under subhead-ings if this helps the sifting process. If, for example, the problem were 'How would you increase the turnover of a restaurant which was doing poor business?', the ideas could be categorised as financial solutions, publicity solutions or service quality solu-tions.

When the ideas have been discussed by the full group, the leader will summarise the conclusions, then link the work that has been done to the session objectives and any assessment.

The activity is very useful for gaining participation. It also stimulates ideas and helps to structure critical thinking. Groups are always pleased to see how many ideas they have when they collaborate. The leader has to impose the structure and channel the energy released in the initial phase.

Buzz groups

In this activity learners are put into pairs to carry out a very small task, usually for no more than 5 minutes, on which they may or may not report back to the teacher/trainer. In its simplest form, people are asked to turn to a neighbour and just talk. No resources are needed. The name comes from the sound generated, which is said to be like that of buzzing bees.

Buzz groups have lots of uses; you can use them to:

- get some ideas flowing before a formal talk or lecture;
- recap what can be remembered of the previous session;
- form a mini-discussion of points raised in a presentation;
- create a safety valve to discharge energy in a long session;
- generate questions to put to a speaker after a talk;
- summarise the main points gained from the session;
- make a start on an assessment task.

Your role is to set up the activity, justify it to the group so that they can see how it helps them to learn, and then use the material which they generate. This last stage can be general, collecting a few points people wish to make, or it can be systematic; you would consult all the groups and comment on their contributions.

Most people are happy to work in pairs; you do not have to move them or any furniture. A surprising amount can be produced and shy people usually join in, as they may not do in a full group.

Discussion

Discussion is a learning strategy which deserves a chapter to itself, so the points which follow are only a trailer to start you thinking. For a discussion, you need to arrange group members so that they can all see each other's faces. This is essential. We don't normally express feelings and argue points to other people's backs. You will also need to prepare students beforehand, telling or negotiating with them the topic, and explaining the ground rules of discussion procedure. You could say:

- everyone has an opportunity to speak; you wait until people have finished before coming in with your points;
- you can criticise other people's ideas and views but not the person themselves;
- the discussion leader will introduce the topic, conduct the discussion so that you cover all sides of the topic, and sum up your main conclusions at the end.

You will need to have thought out beforehand how the discussion will advance the objectives, what content you would like to have covered, who will be the discussion leader, what kind of interventions you will make to keep the discussion on course, and what you will do if it all falls apart. You could take advice from Peter who uses discussion regularly in his communications classes with younger students. Peter has a set of guidelines which include:

- Prepare the students beforehand; use buzz groups for a warm up, no one can discuss productively off the cuff;
- Explain beforehand how the discussion is relevant to the students' work and why they are doing it;
- Tell the students what is expected of them and what your role will be;
- Try not to dominate, this puts them off and makes them lazy;
- Have something else up your sleeve in case this falls flat;

- Don't hesitate to stop the discussion if anyone gets abusive or personal about any other student;
- Always praise their efforts afterwards.

You could use discussion if you wanted to help students develop their communication, interpersonal and thinking skills. If the size of the full group seems fearsome, run discussion in sub-groups, then get one member of each sub-group to report their conclusions to the full group.

Simulation

Simulation requires you to set up a situation in the classroom as similar as possible to a real work or social activity (Figure 6.3). You encourage learners to behave as they would in real life. It is essentially a training exercise in which learners practise the actions, skills and attitudes they will need when they are in the real situation. The following situations are examples:

- an interview for a job;
- an appraisal or redundancy interview;
- handling a complaint in a retail situation;
- a meeting of health care workers to interpret policy;
- a morning's clerical activities in a practice office;
- running the reception desk in a hotel or doctor's surgery.

Simulations are particularly effective for giving insights into sensitive areas such as counselling or guidance, situations where authority has to be handled carefully and for training in any kind of interpersonal skills. However, even an apparently simple situation can arouse all manner of feelings which you must help students to deal with, so you will need to allow plenty of time for debriefing everyone involved. More is said about this in the next section, where your role is described fully.

Role play

This activity differs from simulation in that students in role play situations are

◀ **Figure 6.3**
Simulation prepares students for the real world.

pretending to be people whom they are not planning to be in real life. They are not training to be the people whose roles they play, although they may well occupy that role at some point in their lives. Role play and simulation can be used together. For example, some hairdressing students on an NVQ programme could pretend to be clients visiting a salon, so that the rest of the group could simulate being the real hairdressers who would deal with them.

The purpose of role play is to help learners imagine what it would be like to be in someone else's life or work situation. They might pretend to be unemployed, use a wheelchair, sit on a jury, be a hospital patient, confront a fare dodger and so on.

Although students may not realise it, the 'acting' part of these strategies is only a means to an end. The heart of role play and simulation is in the feedback and evaluation which follow. This takes time and careful management. Below you will find a suggested sequence for managing a simulation or role play session. As you go through it, consider how you could relate it to your group of learners.

Guidelines for managing simulation and role play

- set up the physical environment to reduce distractions and to create an air of reality;
- explain the purpose of the activity, how it relates to the objectives and what students can learn from it;
- brief them thoroughly on what you want them to do;
- brief them on appropriate behaviour, for example, no laughing at or criticising individuals;
- run the activity, noting points you need for feedback;
- close the activity, gather people round, explain that they are no longer in the role play or simulated characters;
- ask students to reflect on how they were in their character and what they have learned;
- lead the feedback from yourself and the group members;
- summarise the learning overall from the session, stressing progress towards objectives;
- thank everyone for their part in the session.

Essentially your role is threefold:

(1) to manage the practicalities of time, place and action;
(2) to manage the sensitivities of the participants;
(3) to manage students' perceptions of what they have learned.

Games and quizzes

It is often possible to turn an exercise into a game, just as you can turn a test into a quiz. Both can be simple affairs which only need writing materials, although they can, of course, be much more elaborate.

Games can be invented or based on existing board or media games such as *Monopoly* or *Trivial Pursuit*. Many students will know the rules of existing games, but do not assume this, and do check whether any students would be distressed about playing because of their religious or moral convictions.

You could invite a group to invent their own game to help them learn part of their programme. A group of NVQ level 2 Catering students invented the one below to help them remember the underpinning knowledge they needed in nutrition.

Make a set of cards showing examples of fats, proteins, carbohydrates, minerals, vitamins. Make another set of cards which show various characters:

- a pregnant woman
- a football pro
- a business woman
- a grandfather
- a mountaineer
- a toddler

Then arrange any five food cards to produce a balanced diet for the person on the card.

This transformed what could have been a very dry set of lists on the board into an enjoyable activity generated by the group. Your role in such activities is usually to brief everyone on the rules and to see fair play; and then to summarise the learning and relate it to the objectives.

Now let's move on to consider activities which work well when you divide a larger group into smaller units. We will look at the nature of the activities and of your own role.

Organising learning activities for sub-groups

Again, these can be simple or more demanding. Usually you set the small groups tasks to perform for which they need the combined resources of their group. You brief them, monitor their activities, then help them convey their findings when they are all gathered together again in the large group.

You can use this approach when you want students to analyse a problem, propose and evaluate solutions, justify actions, compare strategies or engage in other kinds of critical thinking. Most learners enjoy this approach. They feel trusted, and respond well to roles you give them, such as scribe, reporter or chair. You may need to break them into the method over a few sessions, especially if their previous education has been very formal. You should find that quieter people begin to contribute in the smaller group where their voice can be heard.

The quality of thinking in the small group is also higher, in that individuals have more space to think out their ideas and listen to other perspectives. If you ask one small group to present its ideas to another, this will sharpen the critical faculties of each.

Using task-based exercises

You may be wondering what kind of tasks you could set your students to work on.

ACTIVITY | Devise a task which you could give to small groups within your large group. Work out the instructions and how long to allow. Then read through the suggestions which follow for some additional ideas.

Some suggested tasks

(1) Will wants his GNVQ Advanced Construction and the Built Environment group to consider the effects of planning decisions on the local community. He puts them into three small groups, each of which will have to present its ideas to the other two. He gives them a map of a large estate on the outskirts of town and asks them to plan a complete bus route to take account of local features.

(2) Kate is working with rail personnel on an in-house course, tackling the problem of wooing customers on to the trains in off-peak hours. Each sub-group is taking a specific route and brainstorming possibilities in their area. They have to consider cost factors which include potential revenue and marketing costs.

(3) Small groups of GNVQ Intermediate Media students are working with their teacher, Riad, to produce a set of guidelines for respecting the privacy of individuals interviewed for magazine articles. They have to research the legal position in relation to libel as part of their brief.

(4) Karen's Business Administration students are preparing to go on work experience in a range of different firms. Each sub-group is producing a log book format which they could use to record their activities, feelings and skills acquired while in the firm. They will compare their efforts and choose the most appropriate format for actual use.

By now you are probably full of ideas for your own groups. The only limit to this kind of exercise is your own imagination. One form of problem-solving activity which is often set up for small groups is the case study. Let's go on to explore that next.

Using case studies

Basically you set each group a problem to work on. This can be the same problem for each group or each can have a different aspect of the total problem to consider. In the first case, groups would eventually reassemble and compare their solutions. In the second case, they would each report on their part of the solution, with the teacher drawing the whole together at the end. The problem is called a case because it purports to be a real situation requiring attention. Sufficient details are given to create a sense of reality and to make the case complex enough to need considerable debate before solutions will emerge. Case studies can take 10 minutes or 2 days to resolve. That is, you can use a simple outline as a starting point for a discussion, essay or assignment, or you can use a full dossier of documentation which will involve the group in research and consultation. Here is an example of a case outline which you could develop in great detail.

Three parents have come to the head teacher of the school at which their children are pupils, alleging that bullying by staff is going on and asking for an investigation. You are asked to suggest two ways in which the head might respond and the possible implications of each set of tactics. You should consider moral, legal and practical issues.

This scenario could be complicated with details of the school, the staff, the parents and the children if you wanted to turn it into a grander exercise, or it could serve in this form for a brisk discussion period.

It is important in case study work to stress that the **process** of finding solutions is more important than the solution itself. In fact the point is to evaluate several possibilities. There is unlikely to be a single answer or one that satisfies all points of view. This is so in real life, of which the case study is a reflection, and for which it is a preparation.

Your role in managing group activities

Now that you have explored the potential of each of these small and large group activities in some detail, you will be able to appreciate the kind of role which they require you to play.

Although it is your responsibility to manage the overall process, during the activities the students are much more active than you are. You are there to set up the framework, monitor progress, step in if needed, and then help them to draw out the significance of the learning. You could describe your role as facilitation and yourself as a facilitator, someone who eases learners into situations from which they can learn.

You could see this as a series of steps, for example:

- planning the activity;
- alerting anyone else with a role to play;
- arranging the environment;
- explaining the purpose of the activity;
- setting up the sub-groups;
- explaining the task(s);
- agreeing appropriate behaviour in the group setting;
- monitoring progress;
- dealing with disruption;
- coordinating and receiving report back;
- summarising learning in relation to objectives;
- giving feedback on the process of working together.

Let's have a brief look at each of these stages in turn. As you read, visualise yourself working with your own students or trainees. Assuming that you have done your planning and briefed anyone else who may be involved, such as resource centre staff for instance, you are now ready to get the activity under way.

Arranging the environment

You need to decide how you will use the room and its furniture, whether you will need any aids, such as flip chart sheets on which groups can write up ideas, whether you may need to speak to staff in neighbouring rooms about possible noise from yours, whether in fact you need to move to a larger room, and so on.

Explaining the purpose of the activity

This is a very important step. Students will want reassurance that their activities will help them to learn. It is useful to spell this out. They may feel that you are 'taking time off' if you leave them to work on their own in sub-groups, so you will need to explain your own role as well as theirs. You will get some useful feedback, and make them think about their own learning, if you ask them at the end what they thought about learning in this way.

Setting up the sub-groups

Do not be tempted to leave this to chance. You may well want to achieve a particular social mix, to see that some students are restrained and others brought out, or to mix groups by gender, age or cultural background. Work out the composition of the groups beforehand unless you judge it **appropriate** to negotiate or allow free choice.

You can achieve a random mix easily by using this technique. Ask everyone to look at you, then number them round the group from 1 to 4 repeatedly to the last person; then put all the 1s together, all the 2s and so on.

You will probably want group members to take on group work tasks such as chair, scribe or reporter of ideas back to the full group (sometimes called a rapporteur). You may want to determine these, using a rota system over time so that everyone has an opportunity. Make sure they know what the roles imply. Your rapporteurs may be grateful for 5 minutes of the total task time to agree with their group the points to be reported back. Make sure everyone knows what **your** role is before you start, for instance managing the time, checking progress, calling them back together, managing the report back, and summarising the learning at the end. This role briefing is a pre–liminary and separate stage from the step which follows.

Explaining the tasks

It is helpful if you can provide your instructions in writing as well as verbally; this can save a lot of time (the groups may still need help with interpretation). You can give out a briefing sheet or use a board or chart, rather than an OHP which you leave running; the noise and light quickly become irritating. Allow time for questions and clarification in the full group; don't send them off into small groups until they are clear about the task. If students arrive late you can allocate them to a group and ask its chair to do the briefing. This recap will probably help to keep them all on track.

Agreeing appropriate behaviour in the group setting

Some learners may not have worked cooperatively without the teacher's direct con–trol before. You will remember that in Chapter 2 *Getting Started* you looked at the idea of a set of 'ground rules', worked out with the whole class, which they would use to regulate their behaviour. Why not use this exercise now? It may sound as if it will steal valuable time from the main task, but in fact it will save you time later **and** increase the students' respect for the sub-group activities.

Monitoring progress

If you have followed all the steps so far you are unlikely to have any serious problems. Some groups can get a little boisterous when they first try out this method, and the time will come in any group when the task is exhausted and discussion moves on to leisure issues. Your role at this stage is to keep an ear and eye open, while appearing as unobtrusive as possible. You should be 'around', so you can be called in to clarify a point, but not so obviously around that groups feel inhibited (Figure 6.4). Once you have given guidance, move on; otherwise the group will either exploit you to do their thinking for them, or resent you because it looks as if you don't trust them to think for themselves. Be sure to share your attention fairly around all the sub-groups, especially if they are in different rooms.

Dealing with disruption

A number of things can happen to disrupt even the best planned session. It is better to think out **beforehand** what you will do than to be taken by surprise.

ACTIVITY

Look at the list of potentially disruptive events which follows. Work out how you would cope with each. Then consult other staff about their solutions.

● students arrive late or have to leave early, including those with key roles;

▼ **Figure 6.4**
Keeping watch from a distance.

89

- people forget essential materials on which the sub-group is relying, for example, some research findings;
- students refuse to join the sub-groups you have chosen;
- students challenge the task or refuse to do it;
- group members disagree on how to do the task or on opinions about the issues;
- one person dominates/takes over a sub-group.

Don't forget that if you have a set of ground rules, the groups may settle these issues themselves.

Coordinating and receiving report back

Most groups come to this part of the activity with a sense of expectation, looking forward to showing what they have done, and quietly (or indeed noisily) keen for recognition. For you this is quite a responsibility. The secret is good timing.

It is easy to under-estimate the amount of time you will need for report back. Each group must have the same opportunity, which means the same amount of time. If each small group is addressing part of a larger problem, then you must hear adequately from them all in order to cover the content. If they are all considering the same issue, you can avoid the last group having all its points 'stolen' by the others, by asking each group initially to provide only its two main points. Be strict about this. You could easily demotivate one group if you appear to value their contribution less than that of other groups.

As a guide, here is a way you could divide a 1-hour session:

> 5-min introduction to the session objectives;
> 5-min introduction to the activity and how it relates to the objectives;
> 5-min instruction on task and process;
> 10-min task;
> 20-min report back (4 groups × 5 mins);
> 10-min overview and summary of learning, related to objectives;
> 5-min feedback/praise on the way groups have worked together

You can see that the task is the least time-consuming part of the overall activity. However, groups can generate a lot of material in 10 minutes, most of which they will want to pass on. You will need to structure carefully the way they do this, so that they feel a sense of achievement.

Summarising learning in relation to objectives

You need to do this, fairly briskly, because you have the overview and the groups will still be focused on their task(s). You need to present them with the larger picture into which their material fits. This will remind them of the context of the task and help them to 'come down' from the excitement of the group activity. It should also emphasise that they have **learned**, not just enjoyed a period of talking together.

Giving feedback on the process of working together

This is your opportunity to compliment the full group on behaviour which has helped them to learn and to point out behaviour which has caused barriers. You will probably have dealt with any major difficulties at the time in the sub-group(s) where they occurred. Thank the group members for cooperation, for trying out a strategy which may have been new to them, for listening to each other's views and for sharing ideas. Make time to ask them how **they** felt about this way of learning; you will find their views useful in your next round of planning.

You have now worked your way through the key steps in managing learning in small groups.

Summary

In this chapter you have explored the advantages of using group learning activities as a complement to formal presentations and as a valuable learning experience in their own right. You saw how useful group work is in helping learners to develop their interpersonal and communication skills, as well as their attitudes and feelings. You explored strategies such as brainstorming and buzz groups, simulation, discussion and role play, which could be used with full groups. Then you looked at how you could subdivide a large group into sub-groups so that they could work on task-based exercises and case studies.

In the second part of the chapter you investigated your roles and responsibilities in managing full and sub-group activities. You saw how a step-by-step approach would enable both you and your learners to get the most out of this form of learning strategy.

The next area which we are going to consider is the teaching of physical skills. This forms a large part of the workload of many teachers and trainers. In the next chapter you will be able to see how effective skills teaching depends as much on the skills of communication as of instruction.

7 Teaching a Skill

In this chapter you are going to explore the process of instruction, including the methods of demonstration and coaching. This will include teaching and training on courses and in the workplace, and your role in the process of teaching physical skills both to groups of learners and to individuals.

It will quickly become apparent that instructing, demonstrating and coaching have many features in common. You will be able to work through the most significant of these in turn.

Your role in setting up and managing sessions where learners are engaged in practising skills is also explored, together with your responsibilities for health and safety.

A key theme developed throughout the chapter is the importance of your ability to communicate effectively when giving instruction and feedback on progress to learners.

The nature of physical skills

Physical skills involve the coordination of muscles and/or the manipulation of materials, tools and equipment to perform actions. Single skills can be combined with others into larger activities which are called process skills, for example, chopping onions is part of making a complete dish, inputting data can be part of creating a spreadsheet.

Skills are sometimes referred to as 'doing' activities because they involve observable action; they also have an invisible knowledge element and an attitude dimension. To chop onions you need to know what kind of knife to select and how to hold it, and you need to respect your own and others' safety while using it. To input data you need to know the function of the various keys and to respect the confidentiality of the people to whom the data relates.

Physical skills are also called **psychomotor** skills which shows that they combine activity in the brain and in the muscles. When we become fluent in the movements concerned our actions seem 'automatic', we are no longer aware of the brainwork needed. Physical skills rely strongly on the coordination of hand and eye, such as when laying a course of bricks. They also often involve the other senses, taste, hearing and smell, and a sense of balance.

The internal 'feel' which you experience when you perform a skill fluently, when your muscles and senses themselves give you feedback, is referred to as the 'kinaesthetic' sense. This develops gradually and becomes second nature once mastery of the skill has been achieved. It involves dimensions which are difficult to describe exactly, such as pressure, pace, an appreciation of spatial relationships and a sense of colour, which normally only develop over time.

Make a list of those everyday physical skills in which the average person has been trained by the time they are 10 years old, such as tying shoelaces.

Maybe this exercise brought home to you that the learning of physical skills is a familiar part of normal life, especially in our formative years. We learn by copying those around us, from their guidance, by trial and error and by lots of practice. When we learn skills within an educational or work environment, we follow some of these same processes; the teacher or trainer sets the standards for us to achieve, instructs us in the most effective process to follow (thereby cutting out much of the trial and error), and guides us, through the practice period, ever closer to the standards.

Strategies for teaching skills

Instruction is the main process used to teach skills. Two of the methods of instruction which are often used are coaching and demonstrating. Let's look at each of these in turn.

Instructing

This involves an expert telling learners what to do to achieve a particular skill objective. It may be accompanied by a demonstration or the use of illustrative material such as charts, OHP slides or the use of flip chart or whiteboard. It may take place in the work environment or in a training room or classroom. Instructing is often followed by a period of practice where learners apply what they have been told in real or simulated work conditions, such as checking tyre pressures, rescuing a swimmer in difficulties, executing a three-point turn or neutralising hair.

Demonstrating

This involves an expert practitioner modelling a desired way of performing a skill. It is usually followed by an opportunity for learners to try performing the skill for themselves under close supervision, for instance, cooking spaghetti, cleaning down a chain saw or lifting heavy objects; and then by lots of practice.

Coaching

Coaching is usually carried out one-to-one during the job itself or during a period of simulated practice; it involves close attention to the learner's performance, pointing out how it can be adapted or improved. It is intensive and often focused on a part of the skill with which the learner is having difficulty, such as holding the knife for chopping an onion, playing a scale at a particular tempo, inserting a thermometer or playing a backhand ground stroke in tennis.

All three approaches imply considerable follow-on practice by the learners, with and without supervision. Where there is supervision, the learners are given individual feedback on their progress towards acquiring the skill.

All three approaches are teacher centred in that they rely on a structured input from the instructor to provide a stimulus and a model. They are student centred in being designed to meet students' particular learning needs and objectives. After instruction the learners must discover for themselves how to mimic the accuracy, speed and economy of the performance they have been shown. The teacher will help them identify barriers to their progress so that together they can work intensively until a breakthrough is achieved.

You will not find it helpful to think of these three strategies as entirely separate. You will have noticed that they have several features in common, particularly the mix of showing, telling and supervised practice, and the role of the instructor/demonstrator/coach as a model.

Understanding your role as a model

All three strategies are used to provide a model for the learner of what the skilled performance should look and feel like. The 'feel' will come about for the learners after subsequent practice. The teacher identifies all the stages of the skill in sequence, concentrating on each in turn, then links them into a coordinated whole. The learner first copies the steps, then eventually the whole process.

Your aim as teacher is to become progressively redundant, as your learners move towards full competence. Their actions will become automatic, similar to the driver of a car who is able to control the mechanics of driving without conscious thought and concentrate on road conditions and route finding. Eventually learners will go beyond your model to develop flair and a style of their own.

The expert instructor

The demonstrator, instructor or coach is expected to be a model of good practice in their skill area. There are both advantages and disadvantages to this from the **learner's** point of view.

ACTIVITY

Make some points on both sides of the case.
  Here are some suggestions:

For	Against
● Sets the standard	Expertise may be intimidating
● Model to imitate	May pitch level too high
● Enthusiastic style	May go too fast
● Accurate up-to-date content	May be impatient with novice
● Respect for the skill	May not understand learners' difficulties
● Enjoys passing on skill to others	May have inflexible approach
	May be too automatic

The advantages are considerable but the disadvantages could be very serious for the learner. Simply being an expert in your field is insufficient to guarantee that learners will succeed. You may be able to motivate them with your effortless expertise but can you sustain their motivation through their periods of clumsiness and slowness?

The skilled professional **also** needs appropriate skills and attitudes in **teaching** for the effective use of instructional approaches

ACTIVITY

From your experience of being a learner and from observing people learning, identify these skills and attitudes.

Here are some suggestions:

- a positive expectation that learners will succeed;
- keen interest in each learner's progress;
- able to plan sequences of activities which will keep learners interested;
- able to identify individual barriers to learning;
- able to explain in several different ways;
- flexibility of approach to suit different learners' needs;
- patience and persistence;
- sensitive use of feedback;
- more concern for the learners' progress than pleasure in demonstrating their own expertise.

As a teacher of skills you are of course entitled to proper pride in your own expertise, and your students will appreciate your high standards, **as long as** they are used for the purpose of promoting their learning.

Health, safety and welfare

One area in which you need to be a complete model is in relation to health, safety and welfare. Ideally you want your students to adopt your safety code as their own both when they are under your supervision and when they are working on their own. Therefore you need to model the highest standards. Health and safety practices will also be part of the content of your instruction, too, so it is a case both of 'Do as I say' and 'Do as I do'.

There are dangers inherent in the learning of many physical skills. They include:

- damage to yourself;
- damage to other learners;
- damage to equipment, tools, property.

There are potential dangers in both work areas and conventional classrooms, and at any time you may have to respond to an emergency evacuation.

ACTIVITY

Draw up two lists, the first of the potential hazards in a classroom setting (Figure 7.1), the second in the specialist accommodation in which you teach. Include items which affect comfort as well as safety, such as ventilation, and items which would be particularly hazardous for students with disabilities.

◀ **Figure 7.1**
Even an ordinary teaching
room can be dangerous.

In a specialist setting the hazards are more obvious, including laboratory equipment, electricity, gas, water, metals and chemicals. Usually the dangers are well advertised, as by law they must be.

You will be familiar with the health, safety and welfare requirements of your skill area **as a practitioner**, that is, in the work situation. This is different, however, from teaching up to 16 inexpert people in a training environment, or even 2 or 3 in a work situation. Actions and reactions which you can take for granted in experienced workers need to be brought to the front of everyone's mind when novices are working or training.

This fact has implications for your role and conduct, and that of your workplace. Legally everyone has a responsibility for their own safety and a duty of care for that of others.

ACTIVITY

Make yourself a checklist of aspects of health, safety and welfare in your teaching area about which you feel uncertain and intend to find out more. You may need to consult your Health and Safety Officer; you could also talk to colleagues and/or ask to sit in on some of their practical sessions.

The suggestions which follow are only a starting point:

- Induction into Health, Safety and Welfare regulations for staff and students/trainees;
- Insurance protection, including when on work experience;
- Evacuation procedures;
- Registration;
- Leaving trainees unattended;
- Reporting procedures;
- Storage of materials, such as chemicals;
- Length of time trainees can work on equipment;
- Sanctions for infringements.

The need for structure in skills teaching

Although we have all learned some of our everyday skills through trial and error, this is not an efficient or even safe process and not one recommended in teaching.

All teaching involves imposing a degree of order on the mass of raw material available to be learned. Two vital operations are:

- to analyse the whole skill into a number of smaller parts which can be grasped by the learner;
- to put these parts into the best sequence of steps to aid learning.

Many skills are made up of smaller activities, sometimes called skill components, which together make up a continuous flowing performance. If you go and watch a colleague teaching their skill you will be able to appreciate this. Choose a teacher of brickwork, tennis or sugarcraft if you want to notice the grace and economy of overall movement which is made up of numerous separate muscular sequences.

Analysing a skill into its components

Let's use a skill which many people have observed to illustrate this process – shampooing hair. If a teacher of NVQ Level 2 Hairdressing were breaking down the shampooing operation into steps, the list might look like this (notice that some of the operations are interpersonal rather than physical skills):

- Positioning the client;
- Garbing the client;
- Analysing the hair and scalp condition;
- Selecting shampoo type and amount;
- Regulating temperature and flow of water;
- Wetting hair;
- Massaging shampoo into hair;
- Lathering the hair;
- Rinsing the hair;
- Repeating the previous three stages;
- Towelling hair;
- Repositioning client for next process;
- Cleaning up the work station;
- Maintaining communication with the client throughout all stages;
- Working tidily, safely and hygienically at all times;
- Working to time.

ACTIVITY

Now take a skill with which you are familiar. Break it down in the same way as the example above. Notice what you discover.

In the case of the hairdressing example you will have noticed that the parts were sequenced in the order they would be carried out in the salon. This will help the trainees, who will recall the logic of their daily work routines. However, some of the skill components have a knowledge element which will need to be taught first (analysing hair and scalp condition) and communicating with clients will need to be demonstrated and then absorbed through work shadowing and experience. The order in which you teach the skill components may not always be that in which they occur naturally, for instance if you want to ensure that a knowledge and attitudes base is laid down first or of course if you have to wait until resources are available – such as clients with the right hair and scalp conditions.

The process of breaking down the skill into components and then sequencing them is not easy for an expert to whom the coordinated whole has become automatic.

There may, of course, be acceptable variants in sequencing and in operation which you will want to offer to your students once they have grasped the basic routine.

Your communication responsibilities

The teacher's chief tool in promoting learning is language. Although the strategies which we have been examining rely heavily on showing, they need accompanying explanations to draw attention to significant features of action or process, and to relate actions to causes and consequences.

The demonstrator needs a command of language which will convey to people who have not yet experienced it the 'feel' of particular actions; the chef demonstrating blending flour and butter to make a roux for bechamel sauce has to create a picture in words as well as showing the result itself – to describe the desired consistency as 'fine breadcrumbs' is effective because this is a concept already familiar to the learners. He has to convey minute-by-minute changes in consistency, that the learners have not yet experienced. They have to visualise what they will later recognise in fact.

Instructors need language which is specific and imaginative to get over to learners the many sensations which they either have not yet experienced or are not yet capable of recognising – like the changed note of the car engine as you go up the gears, the ease of fabric, the stretch of muscles, the resistance of skin, the pitch of a note. The more comparisons and associations you can invoke through language, the more likely it is that the learners will get the point.

Let's look at four aspects of communication particularly important in skills teaching. These are:

- involving learners in their learning;
- striking the right language level;
- giving unambiguous instructions;
- giving feedback on progress.

Involving learners in their learning

Many learners expect demonstration and instruction to be periods where the teacher does the business while they watch and listen. They adopt a passive role from the outset. You need to change this expectation. You need to get the climate right in which they will ask for clarification, ask and answer questions, volunteer comments or take part in the action. You should begin by showing that you **expect interaction**.

How could you do this? You could begin by rearranging the teaching space (see Figure 7.2).

98

Today's Recipe

ACTIVITY

Now sketch your choice of layout for your next period of
instruction so that students realise that they are expected to take
part in the process.

If you are able to group people round a central table or bench you will set up more
interaction than if you are at a distance, on a podium or barricaded in by machinery.
You may have to resort to gathering people round the end of fixed laboratory
benches. Your students need to be able to see and hear clearly and **you** need to be
able to see all their faces so that you can note anyone in difficulties. Avoid if possible
competition with noisy equipment such as refrigerators or air conditioning systems –
you can shout over the noise but less confident students are unlikely to do so.

You could go on to encourage questions and comments. You could begin by saying
that you'd like questions and follow up by responding positively to the first few that
you get, which will encourage more. If there are times when a question would be out
of order, for example, if you needed to concentrate for safety reasons, you could
promise to come back to it later.

You could go on to ask lots of questions of your own. What you have done so far
will help to set up a climate of trust in which learners are ready to answer your questions. Use open questions which will need explanations rather than one word.

Most of your questions will begin with 'why':

● why do you turn the power off before opening the pressure chamber?
● why do you need to floss teeth as well as brush them?
● why do you move the indicator to the left?

Other useful prompt questions might be:

● when else would you do this?
● what else could you use?
● what would this be in metric/imperial?

- what is the regulation on that procedure?
- when would it not be safe to do that?

Students will often respond enthusiastically to the question, 'What do I do next?', seeing it rather like a game. You could use this question to have them summarise a complete sequence of events as a recap of the session.

You could also encourage students to interact with each other, rather than questioning always being between you and them. Let them explain things to each other, share relevant experiences, point out where to buy materials or equipment, swap tips or cautionary tales.

Learners with particular needs

Many physical skills are well within the powers of people with some degree of disability. To ensure that they are as confident in their learning as other students and that they are as well prepared for assessment, you will need to make additional provision for them during demonstrating and instructing. During coaching you will be able to concentrate fully on their particular skill needs and personal circumstances, adjusting timing, pacing and approach to their situation.

<table>
<tr>
<td>ACTIVITY</td>
<td>

How would you help someone with a hearing or visual impairment or limited mobility benefit from your sessions?
  Here are some suggestions:

- ask the person themselves about their experience to date of studying your subject or related ones; discover from them what they need to help them learn;
- consult a specialist helper in your organisation or ring an advisory body if you want professional help;
- remove as many distractions as possible from the working area, such as sources of noise or obstacles on the floor;
- place them in a position of their choice (Figure 7.3);
- give them the learning materials before the session so that they can prepare;
- encourage them to tape the formal part of the session and times when you are working with them individually;
- provide large print handouts;
- face them while speaking to aid audibility and lip reading;
- make them a priority in the practice period;
- if they choose, get the whole group to work out how to help them and all share the responsibility.

</td>
</tr>
</table>

You are much more likely to draw learners into your session if they feel that you are talking to them about their world. Try to personalise the instruction so that they feel the material is relevant to their learning needs, their work circumstances or their leisure pursuits. It helps if you can show familiarity with their context.

For instance, if you are describing a routine for relief of cancer symptoms to a

mixed group of nurses it is not enough just to refer to public hospital wards, you must also show that you are concerned with private hospitals, hospices, nurses visiting patients at home, those in nursing homes and practice nurses.

Your students will expect you to describe **their** use of the skill. Hairdressers, for instance, work in large departmental stores, small private shops, within the NHS, on cruise ships and in the media.

Use phrases which set individuals right in the context of the work or social scene, for instance

> 'When you move away from the junction . . .'
> 'When you raise the patient in the bed . . .'
> 'When your assailant comes at you for the first time . . .'
> 'While your client gives you her medical history . . .'
> 'When you print out the document . . .'

If you are teaching pre-vocational groups it is very important to describe the skills in context so that individuals can visualise themselves doing the job. This creates a sense of reality and boosts confidence. Learners have to be able to believe in themselves as skilled practitioners whether at operative or manager level. They need every opportunity to see or feel themselves in the right context. This is why it is important to refer to both genders, a wide age range, diverse social and ethnic groups and disabled people when giving examples of people in skill positions. You may also be able to set up realistic work environments and simulations to help learners experience themselves in skilled roles.

You have now created a climate in which learners feel that you are interested and involved in their world, want to teach them and are expecting lively sessions with plenty of interaction. This is a much more promising context for learning than the passive role described at the beginning of this section.

ACTIVITY
Are you sure you know enough about the contexts in which your trainees work or your students hope to apply their skills? Why not arrange to talk to more experienced colleagues or arrange to visit an unfamiliar work environment? You could update your knowledge with a period of work experience or work shadowing.

Striking the right language level

Communicating with learners also means taking their language skills into account. If initial guidance procedures have worked properly, the people in your group should be at the right level for your course or training programme; but you may have individuals who need both your support and that of specialists. Your main task is to refer anyone with difficulties for specialist language help in your own organisation or locally. However, you are the main person communicating with your group and there is plenty you can do in your own sessions to help them. You can:

- check that your pace of delivery is comfortable for learners;
- watch faces for cues to lack of understanding;
- ask if they want you to go over anything again;
- use visual materials or real objects whenever possible;
- label all diagrams clearly;
- explain all jargon;
- write up unfamiliar, foreign or difficult terms;
- provide written versions of any spoken instructions;
- make sure all numbers are written and spoken distinctly;
- ask students to do one thing at a time, for instance, making notes or listening.

Dealing with jargon

Many students find it difficult to learn the tools of their trade. We, as expert practitioners, are so used to our specialist terminology that we don't realise how much of it we are using. We may use abbreviations and acronyms without explaining them – unless a brave student asks for clarification, often to the relief of the whole group.

Specialist words are often long, scientific and based on Greek and Latin terms. This kind of complex vocabulary will not have been common in the previous education of many adult students. Most of the terms are not in everyday use and so are seldom heard. Others **are** in common use but with a general, not specialist, meaning – such as 'bond', 'reconcile', 'seat'. This is very confusing for the learner in the early stages.

You can help by following a series of steps which will gradually make unfamiliar terms familiar. These are:

- use the term in speech;
- demonstrate what it looks like in writing;
- explain its meaning;
- explain where the term derives from, that is, its history;
- relate it to another term which is already known;
- use the term in context;

◄ **Figure 7.4**
Unfamiliar words can be made easier to learn.

- encourage the students to use the term in speech and writing.

Here's an example. This is Hilary, working with her NVQ Level 2 Serving Food and Drink and Food Preparation and Cooking students (see Figure 7.4):

> 'Today we're going to study bacteria, particularly their effect on food, particularly the way they cause food poisoning. The word **bacteria** is plural and refers to several of them – the singular is **bacterium**. The term refers to a large group of tiny organisms, many of which cause disease. The name comes from a Greek word meaning a **rod**. This is because several of these tiny or micro-organisms are rod shaped if you look at them under a microscope. Imagine yourself being caned by a rod if you let any of them into our food in the restaurant. We speak of the **action** of bacteria on food because they are agents which have an active life – although we can't see them at it, because they are so small . . . '.

Giving unambiguous instructions

You have only to think of those instruction leaflets in five languages with minimal diagrams, which accompany a range of products from hosepipes to shelving, to realise the importance of very clear instructions. You have to remember that learners do not yet have a picture of the completed whole lodged in their head, against which to compare the stages of their performance, as you have.

ACTIVITY

You could test your ability to give clear instructions with the following exercise. Write or record the series of steps involved in carrying out an everyday process. Give the list to a colleague who will follow your instructions to complete the task. Then evaluate the helpfulness of your instructions. You could:

- change a fuse
- adjust a lawn mower blade
- make a cup of tea
- log onto the computer
- use a can opener
- check the car oil level

Now write a set of guidelines for a new instructor on giving clear instructions to learners.

Hear are some suggestions. You could:

- begin by saying what it is that everyone is going to learn;
- use sequencing words, such as 'first', 'now', 'next', 'finally';
- avoid padding words, such as 'like', 'you know', 'sort of', 'err';
- avoid dialect and slang terms;
- name parts of objects precisely, for example, 'pass the left lace through the right hole' not 'pass this through that';
- use terms consistently;
- be specific, for example, don't just say 'knife' if you mean 'knife edge', 'blade', 'point' or 'flat';
- be exact about measures; avoid 'a scant', 'about', 'give or take';
- use both metric and imperial measures, if needed;
- separate any anecdotes clearly from your instructions;
- provide a written version of your instructions;
- provide a visual back-up wherever possible.

Demonstration is strongly visual, but if you are working without real materials during a period of instruction, your students will certainly benefit from your use of a flip chart, board, OHTs for diagrams, for example, or charts, pictures or photographs. You may be able to include video clips. Freehand drawings on a whiteboard can show, for example, an overall design, an enlarged version of a small detail or a simplified representation of a complex system, such as a gear box.

Giving feedback on progress

This is a very important aspect of your communication with learners. Many opportunities for giving feedback will occur during the period of supervised practice which usually follows instruction and demonstration, or during coaching sessions.

Some aspects of good practice in giving feedback are the same as those for giving instruction, for example, be unambiguous, be specific. You will see from the next chapter, *Supporting the Individual Learner*, that there are additional characteristics. These include being sensitive to the feelings of the person you are talking to, offering suggestions to learners for improvement and making positive as well as negative points.

Imagine yourself going round the group as it is working on the tasks you have set. What kind of manner and tactics do you think you could adopt, which would create the right atmosphere for giving feedback? Bear in mind that although you are talking to individuals, the rest of the group is close at hand.

When you have thought of some ideas which suit your teaching situation, look ahead to the section on feedback in the next chapter to confirm your views.

Here are some suggestions. You could:

- create an area of confidentiality around the learner – lower your voice, turn your back on other students, stand or sit at an appropriate distance and at their level;
- avoid giving negative feedback in the full group if it would be damaging; arrange to see the student afterwards;
- use each learner's name as you feed back to them;
- tell successful people what they are doing right – they also need specific feedback;
- remember to praise those who are doing well, it is all too easy to concentrate only on those who are struggling;
- move on fairly frequently or you will intimidate individuals by watching them for a long time;
- allow people to correct their own mistakes with your guidance; you will not help them learn by rescuing them.

You will find that students respond more positively to your feedback if you set up the expectation in the first place that mistakes are acceptable because we can all learn from them. You could also point out that learning skills does not involve steady upward progress – we all slip back from time to time or seem to get stuck without apparent reason for a while without moving on. This is quite normal.

Supervising learners while they practise skills

There is little point in being told or shown how to do something unless this is followed very quickly by opportunities for you to practise the skills. Most of us have probably been shown resuscitation techniques but how many of us feel confident to take over in an emergency?

There are four main stages to the period of practice, each of which carries responsibilities for you as a teacher/trainer if you are to ensure that the learners get full benefit from the session. These stages are:

- Setting up the session;
- Observation and monitoring;
- Closing down the session;
- Recording and reporting.

ACTIVITY

Using the headings above, brainstorm ideas on the teacher's responsibilities at each stage.

Here are some suggestions.

Setting up the session

This includes:

- arranging the environment, including checking any equipment;
- establishing the objectives and outcomes of the session;
- briefing people on tasks;
- briefing about ground rules, health and safety factors;
- giving guidelines on timing and pacing;
- explaining your role;
- ensuring everyone understands their role before beginning;
- distributing materials and tools.

This stage is essentially the one where you establish a common purpose and good order. By preparing the environment, checking all materials and equipment, and briefing students thoroughly, you prevent disruption occurring later. Time spent now frees you to concentrate on the **learning** which follows. This is when you determine which students work together or apart, who is responsible for particular tasks, which parts of the work space are off bounds, and so on. In your preparation you will have developed contingency plans for situations you can reasonably anticipate. You will check that any equipment to be used is working correctly and set up safely. You also need to take a register and note any students who missed the instruction period who may need attention at the start; maybe you will pair them off with a more experienced practitioner to make sure they can do no harm until you get to them.

It is essential that you are calm, authoritative and organised during this stage; this establishes the style of working.

Observation and monitoring

During this stage you are both keeping a general eye on everyone and working with individuals. Most teachers of practical subjects seem to have eyes in the back of their heads – teachers of hairdressing find the salon mirrors particularly useful. You also become sensitive to patterns of noise so that you can tell if one group is unnaturally quiet or loud, or if a piece of equipment is malfunctioning.

You will need to set up a pattern of moving around generally, on the look out for people in difficulty or for unsafe situations, alternating with time spent with individuals to check on their progress. You will also be handling any problems to do with equipment – printers not printing out, grills overheating, needles snapping off – and any inappropriate student behaviour, such as not wearing protective clothing or larking about.

You will be keeping a careful eye on the time to see that students keep up the pace of working, particularly if they are responsible for a product – food to sell to the public, for instance – or if you are in an evening class and trying to keep ahead of the caretaker.

Your main task is to give guidance to individual students. This is a skilled operation, of great value to the learner. You will be noticing where each student has got to in the task, whether they have got stuck, or messed up a particular process, or sailed on several stages without difficulty. You will be questioning them about their understanding. In some sessions you may be assessing certain students for their NVQ competences while the rest continue practising.

You may need to demonstrate part of a process to someone who is confused, or coach them in a particular routine – serving vegetables, entering a debit or winding a perm curler. You will be communicating with each person and also with the group as a whole, moving from one mode to the other continuously.

Some teachers are inclined to play down this part of skills teaching, as if it were less important than their more formal activities. In fact it is **the most essential part** for the learner, especially if you are able to give them attention and feedback at regular intervals throughout the session.

The main difficulty for the teacher/instructor during supervision is to allocate attention fairly, to avoid being taken up by one or two students to the exclusion of the rest, either because their need is greater or because they are more demanding. Some teachers try to respond on demand to everyone, which can be frustrating for teachers and students alike.

ACTIVITY

Let's look at this case study. Monica has a computer literacy and information technology (CLAIT) class. She has spent an hour instructing her group in the process of creating and using a spreadsheet. They each have a workbook with exercises. They have already completed the word processing part of the course successfully. They now have a one-hour practice period. She has twelve adult students, three of whom have limited English. One man tries to monopolise her attention throughout the period. He is considerably older than Monica and from a different ethnic group. Two women progress rapidly and keep asking for more work. The rest call out for help frequently, except one very quiet student who seems to have given up. Two young men argue furiously on and off in their own language.

How can Monica manage this session to help everyone make progress? Use your own experience and the pointers given so far to advise her. Try to do this exercise with a colleague.

Closing down the session

Two aspects of the final stage of practical sessions often seem to be in conflict, the need to conclude the **learning** and the need to conclude the **organisation**. The first is all about drawing the threads together, emphasising key points, congratulating the group, setting new goals and targets. The second is about clearing up the room and materials, checking in tools and equipment, and putting things away, all too often in a rush. Both sets of activities are necessary but the second should not dominate or spoil the first. Your main responsibility at this stage is to consolidate the students' learning by summarising the essential points of their performance and understanding while the experience of practice is fresh. Each student needs to go away with an agenda to work on and a clear idea of the next stage of their learning.

Recording and reporting

The most useful thing you can do immediately after the practical session is to make a note of these agendas which you have agreed with the students. It is worth making yourself a chart for this purpose which you can fill in quickly before other activities intervene. You will then have a basis for planning the next session and notes for monitoring tutorials.

You may also need to:

- report on student progress to other staff, such as assessors;
- report faulty equipment or unsafe working conditions;
- report any accidents or incidents.

Teaching skills one-to-one – coaching

Coaching is usually focused on an individual, whereas demonstrating and instructing can equally be carried out with individuals or with groups. In this chapter so far we have looked either at working with the full group or at interacting with individuals during practice sessions in the full group context. Now it is time for you to consider teaching skills to individuals on their own. This is most likely to occur in a work setting, for example, on the ward or in traditional areas of one-to-one instruction such as music, driving, sport, numeracy, literacy or foreign languages. It can of course occur in any skill area as a remedial activity when a student needs additional help.

Let's now look at the dynamics of the one-to-one skill training relationship, your particular responsibilities and some suggestions for good practice.

ACTIVITY	Brainstorm the differences between a group situation and a one-to-one situation for the teaching and learning of physical skills. Some points may seem obvious, for example, that there is only one learner, but they may have several implications for your teaching.

The dynamics of the one-to-one relationship

Most learning takes place within a relationship. In the one-to-one situation the manner adopted by teacher and learner to each other will be very significant. Is the instructor someone from whom the learner feels they can learn? Does the instructor inspire respect for their expertise and for their ability to teach? Can the learner feel 'safe' with them, in that they are going to motivate, encourage and support them rather than criticise and undermine their confidence?

Learners are likely to have certain expectations of their teachers in this one-to-one teaching/learning situation:

- that they will know what it is their learner has to become proficient in, for example, the objectives, syllabus, assessment requirements;
- that they will quickly become familiar with their learner's way of working and understanding;
- that they will adapt their way of explaining to their learner's needs;
- that they will remember the stage each learner has got to from one session to the next;
- that they will not get them confused with other learners;
- that they will treat them as fairly as any other learner;
- that they will provide them with some leadership.

You will also have expectations of the learner, including that they are motivated to learn, will put in effort to do so, will practise between sessions and will use the feedback you give them to improve.

The teaching/learning relationship will be based on this pattern of expectations. If an appreciation of each other's personal qualities and characteristics develops, that is a bonus; the important thing is to establish a professional working relationship.

Your responsibilities in the one-to-one situation

Most of these will be the same as those you have with a group. The difference here is that you have the opportunity to focus all of them on one person. Sometimes we overlook the need to communicate to single learners the things we would tell a group, such as how the sessions are going to be structured, and what the ground rules are. You may even feel that one-to-one sessions don't need planning in the same way as group sessions do, that they will somehow evolve as you both go along. This is an inefficient way of working and rather an insult to the learner. It also means you won't be properly prepared. So . . .

(1) Establish the nature of the contract between you, such as five one-hour sessions, once a week at a set time and place.

(2) Ensure you both have a shared understanding of the goals your learner is trying to meet, whether these are for a relatively short period, such as for improving their bowing, or long term, such as for entering an orchestra.

(3) Discover your learner's current skill level and any difficulties they think they have, either by exploring this with them or by consulting any other staff involved, or both. You will probably do this by getting them to demonstrate a range of relevant activities to you.

(4) Set up a structure for your sessions so your learner knows what to expect, such as revision from the previous session, introduction by you of new skill areas, period of practice with guidance and feedback, or review of learning and target setting for next time.

(5) Find out all you can about your particular learner's way of understanding and performing. Observe their practice closely, ask questions and listen carefully to things said and not said. You will then be able to understand any barriers they come up against and to find ways of explaining and demonstrating to which they can relate. Often it is as simple as finding the right examples and illustrations to chime with their experience and fire their imagination.

(6) Give specific feedback in a positive manner. The one-to-one relationship does not allow you to hide or fudge on issues. You have to speak directly to the learner, who has only your word to rely on. You both need to be clear on the criteria for success and on the degrees to which your learner has met them. This is not incompatible with being positive, offering praise wherever you can, and being encouraging.

(7) Keep a record of the work you do with individuals, it is easy to forget between sessions if you are working with several people in this way. Make yourself a recording/reporting form which allows you to note what you did, what they learned, what was achieved and what the next set of targets is. You may well be asked to report this information to someone else, such as a verifier or senior person at work.

Individual differences

The life experience of each one of us is unique, even though certain general patterns repeat themselves. It is very helpful in one-to-one teaching if you can use each person's experiences positively as an aid to their learning. For instance you can:

- Link the present skill with any existing skill, such as driving a car and riding a bike, breast stroke to back stroke, using a typewriter and using a word processor, or learning Spanish after learning French.
- Link the skill to hobbies or leisure pursuits which may not even be perceived as skills and point out that many basic skills are transferable from one area to another. For example, bird watching can involve making fine discriminations between shapes, patterns, colours and sounds, calculating wind speed and direction, map reading, estimating weather patterns, identifying terrain and vegetation, climbing trees and cliffs, drawing and sketching, and photography, some of which must be useful in other contexts.
- Guard against false expectations and stereotypes. Don't assume, for instance, that older learners will lack confidence or younger ones life experience. Don't expect women to be afraid of technology or men slower to learn cooking skills. Don't expect someone with mobility difficulties to see themselves as disabled. Learners are very quick to pick up your expectations, including those you think you have concealed. The way in which you ask questions, your body language, especially facial expression, can give you away at once. This can get in the way of learning.
- Ask learners how they arrived at a particular conclusion or how they see a relationship – this will provide you with insights into different ways of thinking in your skill area which you have not thought of.

> **ACTIVITY**
>
> Work out for yourself what it would be important for you to get right in a one-to-one teaching/learning relationship in your skill area, given the age, work or life situation of your learners and the nature of your skill.

Teaching one-to-one in the workplace

This situation has great advantages – obvious relevance, response to immediate need, the right conditions and equipment, the work context with all the real sounds and smells. However, there are a few potential problems. If you teach in these circumstances you will probably be able to identify the difficulties quite easily.

(1) Finding time for training

You will have to be disciplined to see that times for training are scheduled and kept to by all those involved; work pressures can so easily take priority because they **are a** priority. Just doing the job is insufficient – there has to be a period of structured reflection on the experience before lasting learning can occur.

(2) Structuring reflection

You will need to create a way for learners to reflect on their learning and evaluate their progress if the routines of work are not to crowd out conscious learning. You could ask trainees to keep a log of critical instances which you review together from time to time. This could complement the practical skill training.

(3) *Extending the job opportunities*
Not all work situations allow you to train staff for the full range of duties or skills needed. You may be limited by the equipment and materials available. This is particularly true of advanced technology. You may also want your trainees to be exposed to a wider range of circumstances than your workplace permits. For instance, in a National Health Service chiropody clinic the clientèle are often over 60 years old exhibiting a limited range of conditions for treatment. You might need to set up job exchange or work shadowing opportunities so that your trainees can cover the full range of skills. You might also use case study examples to broaden the circumstances on which your learner could reflect.

Summary

You have now explored the area of teaching physical skills to individuals and groups in the work and training environment.

You saw that the three approaches of demonstrating, instructing and coaching had a number of features in common. You looked in detail at these strategies, particularly the demands of the one-to-one relationship in coaching. You went on to examine your communication responsibilities in relation to all three strategies and your role in supervising learners when they are practising skills.

You can now explore further your role in working with individuals, this time in a tutorial rather than a teaching/training capacity. In the next chapter, *Supporting the Individual Learner*, we examine the linked processes of monitoring learners' progress and supporting them, practically and emotionally, towards their goals. You will see again how important it is that you are able to communicate sensitively, especially when giving feedback to learners.

8 Supporting the Individual Learner

In this chapter you are going to concentrate on ways of working with individual learners to help them plan, manage and review their learning. The focus of these activities is the tutorial.

You will examine three kinds of tutorial (see Figure 8.1). The first is the action planning tutorial where your role is to give guidance at the beginning of a period of learning. The second is the support tutorial, where your role is to offer the student help with all aspects of their studies. The third is the progress review tutorial where you are involved in helping students monitor and review their learning and achievements, particularly if they are working towards assessment.

Three key aspects explored in the chapter are the need for a systematic approach to tutorial work, the kinds of interpersonal skill needed for a support role and the importance of feedback in the review process.

As you explore the section on action planning, you will be reminded of material in Chapter 2 *Getting Started* and may want to read through this again. The section on monitoring and reviewing progress leads naturally into Chapter 9 *Assessing Achievement*, which follows.

Working with individual learners

Working with individual learners is potentially one of the most rewarding aspects of teaching. Even if you think of yourself as someone who usually works with groups, there may be several occasions when you are relating to one student. Are you involved in any of these activities?

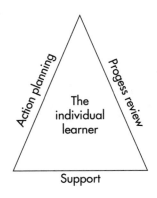

◀ **Figure 8.1**
Supporting the individual learner.

- an initial query/interview for a course;
- an interview for accreditation of prior learning;
- informal time with an individual before or after a session;
- guidance over the telephone;
- an action planning tutorial;
- talking to people one-to-one while circulating in a class;
- a tutorial to review progress;
- written feedback on assessed work or performance;
- a private word about disruption in a class session.

All these occasions represent valuable time when you can concentrate on one person. This is possible even when you are surrounded by others, for instance when you are supervising practice in a workshop. You can be keeping a general eye on everyone, but systematically spending five minutes with each one as you go round. This enables you to check their progress, give feedback and encouragement, and respond to their queries.

The teacher/trainer is almost always trying to balance the needs of the group and those of the individuals in it. This takes considerable organisational and interpersonal skill, which you will learn over time. These skills are well worth learning because successful one-to-one work is very rewarding for both you and your learners.

ACTIVITY | If you have a sympathetic, more experienced colleague, arrange to sit in on one of their tutorials or shadow them within a workshop. Remember to check that this is acceptable to the learners. Take careful note of the teacher's manner and timing.

Not every programme has timetabled one-to-one time. This can be very frustrating for you and the learners. You may find yourself ambushed in the corridor or car park before sessions, or facing an increasingly late departure after class, especially if you teach in the evenings. The solution is **not** to give large amounts of your own time; many students, particularly adults, are adept at making you feel guilty if you don't do this. Resist the pressure, devise inventive ways of using contracted time and do not offer your private telephone number for tutorial use without negotiated and agreed safeguards.

ACTIVITY | Devise strategies for creating one-to-one time within a full group setting.

Here are some suggestions:

- have one session where you give everyone 10 minutes' private time rather than teach; make sure all the rest have something worthwhile to do while you do this;
- make a rota of occasions over a period of weeks where you see two people before the class and two afterwards;
- build in library or learning resource time in which you can see a number of people;
- arrange for a colleague to take the group while you see some of them individually;
- set a task for the group which you review later, during which you talk to individuals.

If you do have programmed tutorial time, you may find yourself using it for one or all of three purposes. These are:

- helping learners plan a course of action to meet their goals;
- helping learners cope with personal problems which are affecting their studies, including poor study skills;
- reviewing achievements in specific task areas.

In the next part of the chapter you can examine some approaches to setting up and managing each of these categories of tutorial. However, in practice these areas overlap, since you are responding to a whole person in whose life the material to be learned, the ways of learning it and themselves as a learner are all interwoven. You will see that it helps you and the learner to have a framework to follow, but, as in most areas of your work, you should aim to be flexible rather than to stick to rigid structures.

Let's turn now to look at the process of action planning.

The action planning tutorial

Nowadays many students have an entitlement to individual tutorial time with a personal tutor. This begins with an induction and continues throughout their programme in a properly planned sequence, including an achievement review at the end of the period. The system is to ensure that learners are on the right programme in the first place and that they are guided and supported during their learning.

Many organisations include tutorials and personal action plans or development plans as part of staff management, training and development.

Let's look at a particular group in a college setting to see how this would work.

A framework for action planning

Aminta is a teacher of fashion design; she is also personal tutor to a group of 16/17-year-old BTEC GNVQ students. Her college has a well-developed support system for personal tutors to help them in their work. Aminta has been given a tutor's pack by the college coordinator of tutoring services, with all the materials she needs to run action planning tutorials.

Aminta's students were all interviewed before enrolling on the course. Her first responsibility is to lead them through an induction process to help them settle into the college (you can look back at Chapter 2 *Getting Started* for details of induction). Some of this will be done with the whole group together, such as drawing up ground rules, introducing them to study facilities and to specialist people who can help them.

An important part of the induction process is to work with each student on a **learning contract** and **action plan**. The learning contract is an agreement made between the student and the tutor (representing the college) about what each will commit to the teaching/learning relationship. Typically it includes references to learning goals and behaviour such as attendance, punctuality and obeying the rules. From the college there is a commitment to teaching, guidance and support as well as to learning resources.

The **action plan** deals with specific learning targets set out in stages as steps towards the planned learning goal (for Aminta's group this will be achievement of the BTEC GNVQ). Progress towards the targets is reviewed in later tutorial sessions, when the action plan can be modified and fresh targets set to suit each learner. This sequence of one-to-one sessions helps both teacher and student 'keep track'.

The tutorials can only succeed if both Aminta and the students have information about their progress; she will have her own records but will need to consult other staff and maybe specialist support tutors before each set of tutorials. Her tutor support coordinator has set all these stages out in a tutorial year planner to help students and staff organise their activities.

The action plans of group members may in fact be very similar, but they will each have made their commitment **individually**.

Now compare this situation with action planning in another kind of organisation.

Hamjit is a community-based chiropodist; he is studying on an in-house programme of professional development, part of which requires him to increase his understanding of the health practices and taboos among ethnic groups in two contrasting demographic areas. He has arranged a tutorial with his supervisor at work to negotiate how he will do this. His own idea is to live with a family in each area for a two-week period. His supervisor will now plan out a programme with him so that he has specific outcomes to work towards and will set dates to see him to review his progress.

Action planning is not just done at the beginning of a period of study; it can be appropriate whenever a significant new start or direction is needed, or when learning needs change. An action planning tutorial could help a learner who has to be absent from a course of study, for instance during a planned period of convalescence after an operation. The tutor and student could set particular targets, including work for assessment to be posted for marking, with telephone tutorials to check progress and give feedback.

Another opportunity for action planning would be before a period of work experience. You can follow this process in the case study which follows.

Going on work experience

Robert is responsible for a BTEC NVQ course in animal care. His group is due for work experience next month; all the arrangements are made. One of the group,

◀ **Figure 8.2**
Action plans need to be followed carefully.

Anne, is very capable in practical situations and has all the right attitudes, but is slightly dyslexic. She will have difficulty keeping the placement diary which is a piece of assessed work. Robert has set up a tutorial to help her cope with this. He is going to accept an audio tape of her experiences and learning rather than a written account. They are meeting for half an hour to agree a structure for Anne's audio diary entries (Figure 8.2), and a review tutorial half way through the placement to check that this method is working. Her action plan is set out on page 117.

Your role in action planning

ACTIVITY

Pick out three significant features of the tutor's role from the preceding discussion and case studies. Then think of ways in which you could develop a role in your particular work area.

Three important responsibilities for the tutor include:

- using a systematic approach to action planning; this includes using proformas on which actions and timescales can be recorded;
- working out the action plan in close consultation with the learner, to ensure that they understand what is expected of them;
- adapting the action plan to the needs and capabilities of the individual learner, which means setting realistic goals which they can reach.

Now let's move on to explore and compare the tutorial framework within which you can support individual learners.

The support tutorial

You will find that students bring a very wide range of situations into tutorials with them, and that study difficulties are often entangled with personal pressures. Here are just four examples:

(1) **Helen**, 17 years old and on a GCSE revision programme (she is trying to improve the grades of four subjects she has already taken at school), tells her tutor that she wants to give up and get a job.

(2) **George**, soon to qualify in a professional examination, wants advice about higher education opportunities where he might be offered academic credit for his existing qualifications.

(3) **Lisa**, due to go on an exchange visit to Spain as part of her City & Guilds GNVQ Intermediate Leisure and Tourism course, is distressed because she cannot find the necessary finance.

(4) **Manjit** returns from work experience in a well-known city firm to say that he has experienced racial harassment about which he would like the college to complain.

We will look at the first of these in detail shortly, but even a brief consideration of the four will help you to see what might be required of you in a support tutor role.

ACTION PLAN

Anne Masters

BTEC NVQ Level 2 in Animal Care

WORK EXPERIENCE ASSESSMENT

This work experience diary will be on audio tape. It will be recorded in each of the four weeks of the placement. There will be six headings which will be used in each recording:

- my regular routine for this week;
- new activities this week;
- significant events (difficult, exciting, special);
- knowledge I have gained;
- skills I have developed;
- particular goals for next week.

I will meet my tutor, Robert, for one hour in week two when he visits my placement; we will play the tape and he will ask me questions. After the placement I will hand in the tape and any writing or drawings which I want to include. Robert will then give me another tutorial to assess my learning.

Signature (Anne)   Date

Signature (Robert)   Date

Your role as a support tutor

Although these cases are typical of the range of situations which can occur, you are not expected to combine the roles of counsellor, social worker and financial advisor with those of teacher. You will find, however, that if you are the one who teaches them, the students will regard you as the first stage of the helping process.

You can opt out of this situation, limiting your activities to teaching and assessment, sending students to other people for guidance. This is a defensible position, though unrewarding for you and the students, and hard to maintain. The reality is that the students' progress is bound up with all manner of academic, personal and work-related issues which cannot be put into rigid compartments. Learning is a messy business, much given to impinging on a person's whole life.

The most useful thing you can do is to follow certain procedures which will help your students to help themselves. Once you have set up the tutorial and agreed any boundaries, such as how much time you will be able to give and the degree of confidentiality required, you can then work through a four-stage process. The stages are listening to the problem, exploring possible solutions, referral if needed, and follow up. Let's go through each of these in turn.

A framework for support tutorials

Listening

Listening implies not just hearing, but making time and mental space to concentrate on one other person **fully** while they confide in you. This is much harder than it sounds, especially as the initial request for help is likely to come in the corridor or as you leave the classroom, when you are surrounded by other people or as you are dashing to the photocopier.

Even when you have cleared a space, found a place and invited your student or trainee to explain how it is you can help, the process will not be linear. It is no use expecting to listen in straight lines.

You can process information much more quickly than the speaker can give it. This enables you to notice a great deal while they are talking. You can listen in three ways:

- to what is said in words;
- to what is said with body language;
- to what is left unsaid.

Listening to what is said

You need to listen actively; this means that you must pick out what seem to be the key points, then check that you are right. Phrases such as

> 'Are you saying that . . . ?'
> 'Am I right that . . . ?'

will help you to keep on the same track.

It is also helpful to summarise from time to time what has been said so far, for example

> 'So you're saying that there are three main reasons for your decision to leave, and they are first of all finance, secondly parental pressure and thirdly the level of work'

Apart from helping you understand the main message, this reflecting and summarising behaviour will reassure the speaker that you are indeed listening.

Listening to how things are said

A tremendous amount of what we understand people to say comes from their non-spoken communication, or the way they are behaving while speaking. Usually this shows us their emotional state and attitudes, either to the subject of the discussion or to ourselves, or both. They cannot help but tell us all manner of additional things which may help us understand more clearly. Feelings such as anger, distress, exhilaration, anxiety, bewilderment will be obvious, but more subtle or mixed emotions may require us to listen with ears and eyes – for example, if the person shakes their head while apparently saying 'yes' to a proposal.

While you listen to the content watch for gestures of hand and head, position of the body, the way the person stands or sits, the pace of delivery and so on.

Listening to what is left unsaid

You may find that certain aspects of a situation are not mentioned. This may indicate that the person is unaware of a major part of a situation or is afraid of it and so avoiding reference to it. You may judge it appropriate to mention this.

Listening is a skill, and needs practice like any other skill; but it is a basic human process, not something exotic which you have to develop to act as a tutor. You will certainly improve your listening skills if you do not:

- assume you know what the other person is going to say;
- jump in before they have time to finish their sentences;
- focus on your favoured solution before they have fully explained the problem.

Exploring possible solutions

The second stage in helping people resolve what they have set out as problems is to move them on to hypothesise about solutions. This is seldom a rapid process, nor should it be. This is the phase during which you can help students to make their own decisions. It is **not** helpful to make these for them. They are the ones who must carry out the decisions and live with the consequences. They are more likely to commit themselves to a course of action which they feel **they** have chosen than one which has come from someone else.

A useful strategy at this point is to raise alternative possibilities and to work through each one looking at the likely consequences. You need to give any factual information which has a bearing on the decision making, or point out that you or the student will need to do this research.

You may find it helps both of you if you set out the possible actions and consequences as a diagram – this also gives the student something to take away and reflect on. This is particularly useful if they are unsettled or distressed.

You have already thought about the case of Helen. In real life you would have much more information than the bare outline here and you would be listening carefully for underlying messages and mixed feelings. Look at the structure which follows to see if it would help you organise the tutorial with Helen in a helpful way.

HELEN

Problem   Wants to leave course and take a job

Reasons

Stated   Financial (wants to earn)
Job prospects no better with qualifications

Unstated   Peer pressure (old school mates are working)
Fear of failure for second time
Problems with GCSE course/staff/group

Possible solutions
1. Leave course and college
2. Hang on till exams
3. Hang on, get part time job
4. Transfer to another course

Consequences
1. No qualifications, poor job prospects
2. Maybe better qualifications, better job but no money now
3. Maybe better prospects, some money, need to fit in job and study
4. Fresh start, hard work, longer overall commitment

Action   Involve parents/guardian
Involve course manager
Involve careers advisor

Now use this structure for situations which you are dealing with or anticipate might be raised by your students.

Referral

It is unlikely that you will have all the information which your students need to make their decisions, nor would this be expected. You **will** know of specialists in the organisation to whom you can refer for help or to whom you can refer your student. This is part of the research you will have done initially when you were considering how to advise potential learners about their learning choices. It is quite in order to send the student on to one or more of these people, though it is often friendlier and more helpful if you make the introductions. The people you are most likely to need will be student advisors on welfare, grants, accommodation and medical issues and careers advisors.

Follow up

You will want to know how your student resolves the problem, so you will follow up with her directly and possibly with those to whom you referred her, unless they tell you that their involvement requires confidentiality. The student needs to know that you are interested in their welfare; most will come back to you in any case to tell you what progress they have made.

It is also part of your professional responsibility to inform your immediate senior or other appropriate colleague of any potentially serious situation involving a learner up to 19 years old; if you are in doubt it is best to report anyway. The Children Act requires you to take certain responsibilities towards learners up to this age in your care. You are also advised to report, even if only informally, in matters involving older learners, if you feel there may be consequences for you or your workplace.

It is always a good idea to make a note immediately after the tutorial of the main points and any decisions or referrals, and to file this record confidentially.

Figure 8.3 (on page 122) shows an example of a simple proforma for recording the main points of a tutorial. It can be used equally well for study-related or personal issues. You can choose whether you want it to be signed by both of you – this is useful if it is to act as a learning or behaviour contract as well as a record.

```
┌─────────────────────────────────────────────────────┐
│                    TUTORIAL LOG                       │
│                                                       │
│                                                       │
│   Name                                                │
│                                                       │
│   Course/programme                                    │
│                                                       │
│   Date                                                │
│                                                       │
│   Brief summary of discussion                         │
│                                                       │
│                                                       │
│                                                       │
│                                                       │
│                                                       │
│                                                       │
│                                                       │
│   Action agreed          By whom         By when      │
│                                                       │
│                                                       │
│                                                       │
│                                                       │
│   Signature(s)                                        │
│                                                       │
│   Copy to                                             │
│                                                       │
└─────────────────────────────────────────────────────┘
```

◀ **Figure 8.3**
It is useful to record tutorial activities.

The progress monitoring tutorial

Your role in monitoring student progress

Most teachers take for granted the idea that they will keep a watch on the progress of their students, discuss their ups and downs with them and nurture them to the end point of their studies. It is one of the frustrations faced by those who teach single sessions that often they have no follow-on contact with the learners.

In the world of National Vocational Qualifications this keeping watch is called **tracking**. When the learner joins a course their details are recorded on a central database. Part of the purpose of this is so that the organisation can claim money for teaching them. In Further Education the money is from the Further Education Funding Council (FEFC); for many training establishments it is from the local Training and Enterprise Council (TEC).

The funding is given on an individual student basis, and is split up into stages. In FE, the college gets money when a student is recruited on to one of its courses. It gets a further payment for guiding and supporting each of them through their studies, and a third sum when they achieve their qualifications or goals.

However, for most teachers tracking means a much more complex and intimate process of monitoring their students' progress than is implied by collecting data. It involves:

- your own assessment of your students' work;
- giving learners feedback on their work;
- giving learners guidance on their study routines;
- talking to others formally and informally about learners' progress;
- keeping records and reporting on learners' achievements.

In the rest of this chapter you will be looking in detail at this kind of monitoring.

Gathering and checking information on progress

Gathering information

First you need to collect your data, gathering together your own observations and those of other staff involved. The data from others may come in various forms – memos, reports, telephone conversations, quick chats in the corridor, assessment documents and so on. The people you consult may be in your work room, in your building, on employers' premises or in other colleges or training centres. It is your responsibility to check that the data which they give you is acceptable as the basis for judgements on your students' progress.

You will need to be sure that:

- all your information is accurate;
- all your information is valid;
- all your information is reliable;
- you have respected confidentiality;
- you have a written record of any verbal report;
- all the information is kept in a secure place.

These points are going to come up again when we explore the process of assessment, and since monitoring progress and giving feedback to learners on their achievements is all part of the assessment process it will help you to work through this set of ideas now.

Accuracy

This speaks for itself. Obviously any information about learners must be correct. You will have to check dates, times, marks, claims, figures and so on. If you don't know all the learners personally, you will need to check very carefully.

Validity

You will want to be sure that any measures of success are indeed checking on the skills or knowledge that you want to pinpoint, and not on something else. Have you checked what you set out to check, and were these the right skills, knowledge and understanding to check in the first place?

Imagine you are checking on the progress of a hairdressing student; everyone says he is such a pleasant person – yet when you look closely you see that focus on personality has led people to overlook slipshod practical work. Both personality and accuracy are important, but be sure you know which one it is that you are focusing on at the given time.

Another example to illustrate validity might be if you were checking a student's knowledge of how an internal combustion engine works through a written account. The facts are all there, but the level of grammar and spelling are poor. You need to be sure that the credit you give is for the knowledge, not the English, **unless** grammatical expression was a requirement of the test. You might also consider whether a written account is the most appropriate measure of understanding.

Reliability

Usually assessment will be reliable if it is based on criteria which are used consistently by assessors, but differences of interpretation of criteria between assessors in some subject areas are difficult to control. You will want to talk to other people involved to check that your interpretations are as close as possible to those intended.

Confidentiality

Many teachers talk informally to each other about their students as a way of weighing up their progress. But they are careful not to do so when other students are present, or to leave written reports about where they might be seen by the wrong people. It may be that a student has confided in you the personal reasons why they are not making much progress at present. This is helpful for you and them, but it is not appropriate information to pass on to other people at this stage, if at all.

Written records

It is much easier to pick up the telephone to pass on information to a colleague but much more reliable, accurate and confidential if the report can be written and passed on in a sealed envelope. If you receive information over the 'phone it is tempting to think that you will remember it accurately, but it is in fact very unlikely. The quick word in the corridor or over the 'phone needs to be turned into a written record as soon as possible.

Security of information

You also need to keep your records in a safe place – this is not your briefcase or the back seat of the car. Briefcases are easily left on trains and cars broken into or papers in them chewed by children or dogs. If possible records should stay on the premises in the workplace, whether on disc or in a file drawer. Part time staff are entitled to ask for space for this.

Internal verification

If you are working on an NVQ or a GNVQ programme you will be asked to record information about individuals' progress in a particular way, using forms produced by your workplace or awarding body for this purpose. Usually this is a brief record of units of achievement (parts of the programme which have been passed) gained by each person. This will be backed up by other assessment information such as checklists or short written reports.

All of these will be checked by a person appointed within your workplace as an internal verifier. Their role is to check that you are acting as an assessor should, that your records are accurate, that your judgements are appropriate and reliable, and that therefore your learners are being treated fairly. You will be briefed by your internal verifier about the verification process, so that you can follow it from the beginning.

ACTIVITY	Arrange to see the internal verifier for your area of work; ask for a briefing. If your work area does not yet have NVQs or GNVQs, search out an internal verifier in a related area who will describe the system for you.

A framework for monitoring and review tutorials

It is best to approach monitoring and review systematically for the sake of both the student and yourself. Regular dates for review sessions will help students manage their learning. Many programmes have in-built assessment deadlines; if yours does not, it might be useful to create some. An imposed structure may be resisted but is unlikely to be resented – it is too obviously useful. With some students you may be able to negotiate a pattern of assessment deadlines and review dates, using the learning contract and action planning process you looked at at the beginning of this chapter.

Setting up the sessions

(1) About two weeks before the event, remind the students of the date, the agenda and the logistics. Give clear guidelines on your role and theirs. Outline preparation needed. Give these details face to face and in writing.
(2) Make contingency plans for disruption, such as lateness.
(3) Arrange suitable accommodation – quiet surroundings, no 'phone.
(4) Make suitable arrangements for any student with a disability, such as access for a wheelchair user, or tape recorder for a visually impaired student.
(5) Collect all the assessment information you need.
(6) Create a plan for the review process with approximate timings for the stages. This might look like this:

> **Review session** with **Sharon Mitchell**
> 16.09.96. 0900–1000
> GCSE in Computer Studies
> Computer Applications
> Binary, Decimal and Hexadecimal systems
>
> 0900 Outline purpose and procedure of the session
> 0910 Review assessment requirements

0915 Go through student's material for 1st term project
0925 Highlight areas for further development (if any)
0935 Check plans for next stage of work
0945 Any questions or other areas for discussion

If yours is an NVQ programme you could work through each element of the unit in turn, if that is appropriate, checking the student's progress in producing the required evidence, before looking at their organising and cross-referencing of it.

ACTIVITY

Produce a set of briefing notes for students whom you will see individually for review, in which you explain the purpose and the arrangements for the session.

During the review session

To some degree you will have to respond to how the student deals with the session, so stages and times are a guide rather than a straitjacket. However, if you have several people to see you will need to be quite disciplined. You could begin by setting boundaries, for instance reminding the student of the purpose and format of the session and the amount of time available. You are there to review progress. If they have other matters which they wish to raise, you could arrange another appointment to deal with those issues. Follow your plan as far as possible, using a watch or clock unobtrusively. Listen as well as talk, use your records and notes to give them feedback on their progress, encourage questions and check that your points have been understood. At the close you will need to set goals for the next stage of work and log your decisions.

Giving feedback on progress

Feedback is the key to progress. In the review tutorial you will be giving your students the feedback information they need to appreciate the extent of their achievements and any renewed efforts which they have to make. Without this thoughtful, regular guidance they will find it difficult to progress. It is a major part of your role, whether or not the student then goes on to formal assessment.

Information given to learners about their achievements up to the point of final assessment is called formative feedback. It is called formative because it forms or moulds the direction of the learning towards a desired standard, level and goal. You have in your mind a picture of the required performance which you try to put into your student's head through the process of giving feedback.

Feedback is by its nature specific to the individual. It is a very personal matter. Each learner has his or her self-esteem bound up in the learning process. Fear of failure is not only a spur to greater efforts, it is a spur to giving up. You need to be aware when you teach or assess that the way you give feedback is as important as the fact that you give it. However objective the feedback, the learner may have difficulty receiving it, even if it is positive. Some learners have too low a self-image to think well of themselves. A 'don't care' attitude to negative feedback may mask considerable distress. The review tutorial gives you a private opportunity to handle this delicate process.

Imagine that you are advising a new teacher/trainer in the business of giving feedback, in class or in tutorials. Suggest 10 points which they should aim to follow.

Good practice in giving feedback

- Be positive: always find something constructive to say even when the overall message is negative.
- Be specific: relate praise or criticism to the actual points at issue.
- Be personal: look at the learner, use their name, refer to their work.
- Be tactful: choose a private place to make comments.
- Be honest: give a straight message as the basis for improvement.
- Be attentive: watch how the feedback is received.
- Be sure: check that your student has understood your points before proceeding.
- Be patient: be prepared to explain your points more than once.
- Be creative: suggest how work could be improved.
- Be realistic: set new goals which are achievable in the short term.
- Be confidential: hold tutorials in private, put written statements in envelopes, keep files locked away.

After the review tutorial

It is best to make any notes as soon as you finish; you may need to allow a small gap of time for this if you are seeing a series of individuals.

You can use your record sheet to note points to follow up. You may need to pass information on to others such as student support staff, other assessors or your internal verifier. Make sure you keep your notes in a secure, confidential place.

When there is an appropriate time, ask your students for feedback on the way you conducted the review tutorials. If this is too difficult for them, maybe you could audio tape a session. They may find it hard to tell you directly because of the one-to-one nature of the activity, but you do need the feedback if **you** are to improve.

Summary

In this chapter you have explored three kinds of one-to-one session, the action planning tutorial, the support tutorial and the progress review tutorial. In each case you looked at an appropriate framework for the tutorial and at your own role. You noted in all three cases the need for a structured approach, and the need for a sensitive response to the individual needs of each learner.

Progress review leads naturally to a consideration of assessment, which is the subject of the next chapter.

9 Assessing Achievement

In this chapter we are going to explore the process of measuring the extent and quality of your students' learning, the process of assessment. Assessment is at the heart of learning – when you carry out assessment you and your students are able to judge how successful they have been in progressing towards the goals which they set themselves. This is true, whether your work involves giving apparently casual feedback to people in leisure learning situations or setting tests in formal or examination conditions, or assessing performance in the workplace.

Many of you will be taking one or both of the Vocational Assessor Award units D32 and D33 with their highly specific requirements. No attempt is made here to reproduce or rephrase the guidance found in the standards themselves, although both the mechanics and spirit of assessing competence-based learning, directly and with other people, are included.

As you work through the chapter you will be introduced to key concepts, specialist vocabulary, formal and less formal contexts, and traditional and competence-based schemes, much of it through the actions of a series of teachers used as examples.

Your role in assessment

Assessment is currently both fashionable and contentious; there is a great deal of attention on testing school children's attainment at certain ages, on the rising or falling of standards of GCE A-levels and GCSE and on creating new competence-based vocational training and further education qualifications (NVQs and GNVQs).

This degree of emphasis on assessment has tended to distract attention from what many teachers see as their main role, that is, teaching or helping people to learn.

In fact, teachers are assessing all the time. Every time you ask a question of a class or an individual you are assessing their knowledge and understanding. When you walk round the workshop or workplace watching people welding surfaces or wiring circuits you are observing and noting against a checklist of expectations in your head. When you listen to a discussion which you have set up, or receive the report back from a syndicate group, you are comparing their performance with that which you would hope for from such a group or individual at such a stage in such a course at such a level. Your nods, raised eyebrows, affirming smile, restraining hand give volumes of unspoken feedback.

You will have based your teaching on what your students need to know, understand, perform, feel, demonstrate, exemplify – their objectives – to meet the demands of their eventual assessment; each time you teach, you monitor their progress. Listen to your reply to a colleague who asks how a particular student is progressing, and you will realise how much assessment data you have stored away, even after only a few sessions.

Assessment is not an activity reserved for special, formal occasions. It can take place informally throughout your regular teaching – through question and answer, observation and listening.

You can see that assessment, although a separate stage of the teaching/training cycle, is also closely linked to every other stage of it.

ACTIVITY

Show how assessing is linked to identifying learning needs, planning learning, delivery, and evaluating teaching.

At the **needs** stage you establish your students' goals and the particular objectives which they will aim to meet. These objectives form the basis of the assessment scheme; this is the most direct link between stages.

At the **planning** stage you work out the routes the students will take to become competent and confident in the activities referred to in the objectives. You also plan opportunities to monitor and review their progress and give them feedback; this is formative assessment. Whereas much of the learning will be for its own sake and there will be all manner of unexpected spin-offs, a major purpose of your planned programme is to prepare the learners for assessment.

At the **delivery** stage you use teaching and learning strategies most suited to helping the learners meet their objectives, you assess their learning informally and give them feedback.

At the **evaluation** stage you use the results of your informal and formal assessment to judge how well **you** have done at all the other stages, including the assessment stage. You see how well **you** did by seeing how well **they** did.

Assessment in theory

Before we go any further, you need to check your understanding of some of the concepts and terms used in discussing assessment in theory and practice. The next part of this chapter will be a *brief* summary of the main ideas, which you can then see exemplified in the case of studies of teachers in action as assessors which follow.

When you assess students' activities you compare their attainment with a standard that you or someone else has laid down as appropriate for the qualification or level of achievement being sought. There are several reasons why you might do this.

Purposes of assessment

ACTIVITY

List your ideas about the purposes of assessment.
  Here are some suggestions:

(1) To measure learners' progress towards a goal so that you can give them feedback to help them improve – **formative assessment**.

(2) To diagnose areas of strength and weakness in their work so that you can help them work on their difficulties or change your teaching programme and methods if that is where the problem lies – **diagnostic assessment**.

(3) To make a judgement about their final level of attainment – **summative assessment**. This means you sum up the end point of the learning. Summative assessment does not only take place at the end of a learning programme. When it does it is sometimes called **terminal assessment**. If a programme of learning is modular or in blocks, each of which is assessed by an assignment or activity which is not revisited, then each of these assessments is summative. This approach overall is called **continuous assessment**.

(4) To **predict** how an individual might succeed in a future course or occupation or particular situation, based on the inferences you draw from the test results.

(5) To **compare** one student with another, to place them in rank order. You can review the order for a group overall or how members cluster between certain cut-off points in the marks. These categories or **grades** can be made to express degrees of capability in terms such as distinction, merit or in letters, such as A, B, C. The results can be used to **select** successful students for particular jobs or other types of education.

(6) To **motivate** students, to show them they are doing well, or to stimulate them to try harder in order to avoid failure.

Key concepts in assessment

The standards for comparison

There are different kinds of standard with which you can compare your learners:

(1) You can compare their performance with a set of criteria which represent 100% or total achievement at that level – **criterion referenced standards**. This kind of achievement is also called **mastery** since you achieve complete competence in the subject concerned. There is no grade other than **pass/fail** for this kind of standard. National Vocational Qualifications are based on this principle – so is the driving test.

(2) You can compare their achievement with a standard that is the normal one expected in that kind of test or examination at that level – **norm referenced assessment**. Large national examinations such as GCE A-levels are norm referenced. The norms are arrived at by piloting a test on hundreds of suitable people and establishing the range of levels of achievement. This is called **standardising the test**.

(3) You can compare their achievement with their own previous standard – **self-referenced assessment**. This approach is suited to testing development of attitudes and values where there is no absolute standard, such as enterprise or confidence, and for people who may only be able to achieve very small steps judged by conventional tests.

Types of test and types of evidence

One of the skills of assessing achievement is to use the right test for the job. Different tests are good for different purposes just as some are plainly unsuitable – you would not use a written test to judge someone's competence to pilot a plane. When you are assessing you are looking for proof or **evidence** of the person's capabilities.

Evidence can come in several forms – it can be written, visual, oral, actual performance and so on. You need to match up the purpose of your assessment with the type of test which will produce the evidence you need – such as using a practical performance test to see if a trainee driver can handle a car.

ACTIVITY

List the ways in which **you** could be convinced that a trainee or student was competent (assuming that you yourself are competent in the same subject or skill area).

- you could observe them in action;
- some other qualified person could observe them and give you a report;
- they could be videoed in action and give you the tape;
- you could question them;
- you could ask them for written material;
- they could be audio taped in action and give you the tape;
- you could look at materials or objects they had chosen/created/assembled/decorated;
- you could ask supervisors at work to vouch for them;
- you could ask their clients/patients/students to vouch for them.

ACTIVITY

Now brainstorm all the kinds of tests you have experienced or heard of. Jot them down just as they occur to you.
Here are some suggestions:

- formal written examinations in limited time;
- pen and paper tests (informal);
- short answer tests (written);
- oral tests, for example, in language learning;
- question and answer;
- interview;
- viva voce;
- quizzes;
- projects;
- assignments;
- case studies;
- oral presentations;
- practical performance test – how to do or make;
- product of practical test – things done or made;
- simulation of real performance, such as operating aircraft controls;

- written exams with questions beforehand/books to consult;
- drawing and graphic representation tests;
- aural tests (listening and responding);
- objective tests – multiple choice and others;
- coursework

and so on.

The purpose of these two activities is to show you that there are many different methods of assessment from which you can choose, which will interest and motivate your students as well as test them. Think of their changed attitude to a test if you were to repackage it as a quizz, using formal rules and procedures to give it credibility.

Characteristics of effective assessment

There are two important criteria which are applied to test situations and to **assessment instruments,** as tests are called. These are the concepts of **validity** and **reliability**.

Validity refers to the ability of the test to do what it is supposed to do. If it is supposed to test understanding and application of knowledge, does it do so or does it test only memorisation and recall? If it should discriminate between those students who are really proficient and those who are only marginally proficient, does it do so or do they all get much the same marks? If you want to test interpersonal skills and you give a written test, you are not going to learn what the students are like in action – this is an invalid test. So you need to find or create a test which is fit for its purpose.

Reliability means you can trust the test. If you used it to test the same student a second time you should get the same results, or the same spread of results if used on the same group (assuming they do not practise or consult anything in the meantime). If another assessor used it they should get the same results as you. Criterion-based tests are likely to be more reliable than those allowing considerable interpretation of the questions. Objective tests, where there is only one right answer, are highly reliable. But although they may be reliable in themselves they may not be a valid way of testing for a particular set of skills and attitudes – counselling and guidance skills, for example.

There is much more to explore about both these concepts but not in this summary – you will analyse them further later in the chapter. You need now to look briefly at four other criteria of test effectiveness which apply to all tests and particularly to NVQs and GNVQs.

Authenticity

This is so obvious it hardly needs saying. Is the evidence the person's own work? Has it been produced unaided? Much of the formality of large public examinations, where the accent is on memorisation rather than original thinking, is designed to ensure there is no cheating. It is vital when assessing coursework, projects and assignments, and when evidence is brought forward for the accreditation of prior learning, to have ways of checking for authenticity.

Recency

This term refers to the currency of the material being presented for assessment, particularly written work and submissions for accreditation of prior learning. It is important in subject areas where it is essential that people are fully up to date, such as First Aid or Computing. You will need to check that any knowledge and skills claimed from previous experience or through certificates are still valid.

Sufficiency

Basically, is it enough? Are you convinced? Does the material cover the range of applications, are the skills demonstrated often enough to show competence and not fluke or coincidence? All assessment is based on sampling. Have you sampled enough to be sure that your learner is competent?

These three criteria are powerful in combination with each other, and with validity and reliability, in determining that a test instrument or situation will be effective.

Fairness

All these requirements contribute to an overall criterion of **fairness**. Many parts of the assessment industry are working to ensure fair, unbiased and equal treatment for all candidates for assessment. Is the assessment opportunity equally open? Are the rules the same for everyone? Is the assessor competent?

ACTIVITY	Read this small case study, then think about ways in which this situation could discriminate against members of the group.
	The first assignment on an Access to Higher Education (Social Sciences) course for mature student returners involves going to the college library, finding information on current law and order issues in the UK, writing a short report and then giving a short presentation to the rest of the class.

This assignment would daunt an established group of students with the necessary familiarity with the library, study skills and confidence in talking to each other. A new group:

- may not have the skills of information retrieval or the confidence to ask for help;
- may not understand the concept of law and order sufficiently to find the information;
- may be nervous of expressing unfamiliar ideas in writing without guidance;
- may not have the language skills or confidence to speak in public among relative strangers.

There are also issues of inappropriate timing, lack of preparation time, and unsuitability of this combination of assessment methods.

Assessment in action

Your responsibilities in the assessment process

Let's now look in detail at your specific responsibilities.

ACTIVITY

Use the questions below as your guide to an initial analysis:

Whose work do you assess?
(type of learner, age, number, gender)
What do you assess?
(subject area, skill, theory, practice)
What kinds of learning do you assess?
(performance, knowledge, skill, attitudes, values)
Why do you assess?
(give feedback, motivate, prepare for qualifications)
How do you assess?
(practical, oral, written)
When do you assess?
(all the time, from time to time, at the end)
Who provides the tests?
(you, awarding body, institution)
Who recommends the level of success of candidates?
(you, internal verifier, external examiner)
Who gives the candidates feedback on how they have done?
(you, external examiner, exam board)

You may find that your situation is very different from that of colleagues. This is to be expected. Further and Adult Education and Training covers a very wide range of students and courses with an equally diverse range of approaches to assessment. Here is a description of some of the members of a typical teacher training group to show you some of that range:

James   teaches and assesses in Grounds Care and Maintenance. Uses observation of performance, mainly use and care of equipment. Has assessment checklists. 100% pass needed to ensure safety.

Catherine   teaches and assesses for BTEC certification in Animal Care; uses projects which are mainly practical plus objective tests. Her work is checked by a moderator.

Robin   teaches Accountancy evening class students mainly running own small businesses. Prepares them for external exam by using lots of written exercises from past papers.

Gerald   teaches techniques of Bereavement Counselling and assesses with a colleague using observation of practice and a student self-assessed journal.

Monica   teaches computing to adult trainees aiming to return to work. Assesses as part of a team who use an integrated RSA scheme. Judgements checked by an external verifier.

Jacqui   teaches Yoga on an in-house hospital programme for nurses. No formal assessment but uses recommended British Wheel of Yoga standards to give formative feedback.

Fran   teaches self-help cookery to adults with moderate learning difficulties. No formal assessment but keeps records of their progress in relation to their previous level of competence.

Nicholas   teaches French Language and Literature GCE A-level. Prepares students for external exams, oral, aural and written. Uses past papers and subject specialist conferences as a guide to levels and grades.

Carol   teaches and assesses City & Guilds NVQ Level 3 Hairdressing. Follows set assessment procedures and criteria. Uses observation of practice in a realistic work environment (college salon) with questioning and written tests set by City & Guilds.

Barbara   trains radiologists for a breast screening service attached to a hospital, and uses external exam standards to give formative feedback on practical technical and interpersonal skills.

Wanda   teaches sugar skills to beginners adult evening class and assesses informally through observation of practice and questioning, using her own criteria. Makes all her own decisions, no supervision.

ACTIVITY

Now that you have been introduced to this group of peers, look back over your own role description to compare it with theirs. As a further step, look back over the Assessment in theory section to see which of the concepts, techniques and approaches applies to which members of this group. You could ask:

- who is mainly concerned with giving formative feedback?
- who does the assessment but has their judgements checked by both internal and external colleagues?
- who has to create their own assessment instruments but has guidance from an awarding body (City & Guilds, RSA, BTEC, professional bodies)?
- who is left to make their own decisions with no guidance?
- who is working to national norm referenced standards with graded results?
- who is training students in the workplace and assessing them in their job?
- who is using a simulated working environment sufficiently like the real thing to be acceptable for assessment?
- who has no feedback about their individual students' performance in the actual examination?
- who works in a team to create assessment instruments?
- whose students must meet every criterion in their tests?
- who is assessing relationships as well as technical skills?

Case studies in validity and reliability

Let's now explore the work of four of these teachers in more detail in order to take the ideas of validity and reliability, authenticity, sufficiency, recency and fairness a little further. First here is some extra information on the last four of the group, Nicholas, Carol, Barbara and Wanda:

Nicholas (French Literature and Language GCE A-level) is teaching a wide range of skills – speaking, listening, reading, writing, comprehension, application, analysis and evaluation, all requiring a degree of recall, for example, of vocabulary, grammar rules, or rules of literary criticism. He needs to develop student confidence and foster an appreciation of the culture to which the language relates.

Such a range of skills involves a range of oral, aural and written tests, some requiring an immediate response, some allowing time to reflect and form conclusions. He gets guidance on standards and approaches from other members of the language team, from past examination papers and from the annual Chief Examiner's Report. He has a model to which he can work closely. He uses this to produce practice assessments throughout the year and mock examinations. He holds an MA in French but does not have to be qualified as an assessor.

ACTIVITY

Let's look at how **valid** and **reliable** Nicholas' assessments are likely to be. You saw earlier that a valid test was one that was fit for its purpose and did what it was supposed to do. Ask yourself if the combination of tests used by Nicholas is suitable, if it matches the skills and knowledge he needs to test. Reliability meant that the results arising from the testing could be trusted – what would lead you to trust or doubt the Nicholas situation?

Nicholas

Validity

Nicholas' assessment situation has high validity. He is modelling his own tests on nationally approved models – the students will be well prepared for the real thing. He copies the range of tests, assessing fluency in speaking by oral tests and in listening with comprehension by aural tests. He uses essay style questions for the literature. This is a good match.

Reliability

Nicholas is relying on colleagues and the Examiner's Report for the standards the students should meet, but he is not a trained assessor. A more experienced colleague should check his marking in the practice tests and mocks since A-level involves interpretation, not just recall and application. Regular meetings of this nature would guarantee reliability, though it is probably quite high because of guidance from the Report.

ACTIVITY

Now do the same exercise for the remaining assessors – Carol, Barbara and Sandra.

Carol

Carol (NVQ Level 3 Hairdressing) is working in a highly structured, carefully controlled assessment situation. All the criteria on which she must make a judgement are given to her and to the students by the awarding body (City & Guilds). She has to explain and interpret the criteria and show the students how to put together a portfolio of evidence to prove their competence. She works closely with the other members of the staff team, who share the assessing.

Her methods are observation of her students at work in a simulated work situation, a practice salon open to the public. She uses a checklist of assessment criteria during observation of their practical work, questions them on their understanding, sets and marks written short answer and multiple choice tests. She can give immediate feedback to the students on strengths and weaknesses. If they have elected to go for assessment in a particular process before they are really ready she can advise them to wait, or, in the event of failure in part of the work, arrange remedial work and a new assessment date. She herself is a qualified assessor (Vocational Assessor's Award D32 and D33) and her judgements are checked by an internal verifier member of her section and an external verifier from City & Guilds.

Validity

This situation has high validity. Observation of live performance checks on practical skills, questioning to the individual checks on understanding and on the application of the various skills in situations which cannot be covered live in the salon. Written tests requiring limited answers deal with recall of factual theory information. The assessment checklists ensure that the content of the assessment matches the objectives of the learning. There is a strong match. The match would be stronger in the workplace itself with real clients and a faster work pace.

Reliability

This is very high. National standards are used, everyone is working to the same criteria, the assessor is trained in assessing NVQs, the assessments are checked internally and externally.

Barbara

Barbara supervises three trainees every six months while they are on placement in the breast screening clinic; they are already fully qualified nurses. They will be assessed by means of an externally set and marked practical and theory examination (College of Radiographers in conjunction with a university). Barbara prepares them for the practical work of managing the patients and handling the screening and photographic equipment. She works with them individually and as a group. She briefs them on their tasks, gives them practice through simulations, then supervises them using a checklist of criteria while they work with real patients. She gives each one detailed feedback and encourages the group to assess each other. She is an expert in her job but not a qualified assessor. She herself is supervised by her line manager who sits in on sample training sessions.

Validity

Here again appropriate forms of test are used – performance is observed, understanding is questioned and it is in a real work environment. The criteria used relate to the objectives to be met. Encouraging trainees to assess each other helps them incorporate the criteria into their own behaviour. This approach should prepare trainees well for the external examination.

Reliability

Barbara is an experienced worker and versed in the demands of the examining body. She is also supervised. Her interpretation of what is needed should be reliable. She will also know from the patients when the training is working or if anything needs amending. She might be biased by her familiarity with the trainees but she uses written criteria to avoid this and has her judgements moderated by student and line manager.

Wanda

Wanda's group (Sugar Skills for Beginners) attend the course wanting feedback but not wanting formal assessment. They have come to learn the skills, not to be examined in them. Since they do want to know about their progress, Wanda has produced a checklist of skill indicators which she has shared with the group. She uses these when observing their practical work and scrutinising their finished products. She asks questions to check their understanding of products and processes while she is demonstrating to the group. She listens to what they volunteer as she goes round the class observing. No one else is involved at any point. Although she is an expert in sugar skills, Wanda is not yet qualified as an assessor but she has begun training for the Vocational Assessor unit D32.

Validity

Wanda's approach has high validity in that it suits the students' needs and expectations, and produces feedback of a systematic nature against a list of criteria that is known and explained. She assesses practical work by observation and understanding by questioning. Written tests would be unsuitable for the group or the subject at this level.

Reliability

The assessment situation is reliable to the extent that Wanda is a subject expert who is likely to know what she is looking for and to recognise it when she sees it. It is unreliable in that she has devised the criteria without consultation or guidance; she may not have estimated beginners' level accurately and the students cannot tell this. There are no checks on bias in the use of the checklist, although its existence and openness is systematic and so aids reliability.

You can see that there is much to debate here and not all situations are cut and dried. Generally, validity is most likely when tests match in content, level and form the objectives they are supposed to assess within a particular context – the right test for the right job. Reliability is most likely when clearly expressed criteria with agreed interpretations are used in the same way by trained assessors who are also subject specialists, and there are systems for checking assessors' judgements.

Authenticity, sufficiency and recency

These are much easier to determine and in the case of these four assessors they are all working face to face with their students or trainees. Written work is the most likely test to be suspect unless done face to face with the assessor; project work needs most checking, especially where it is required only in written form or is the only form of assessment. If any of Carol's hairdressing students had been asking for skills demonstrated previously to be accepted without further proof, she would have had to check on the reliability of the previous assessor's judgement, including checking on the authenticity of any certificates offered as proof of competence.

The four assessors also worked with their students over time and had the opportunity to collect enough of the evidence they needed. Both Carol and Barbara would need to ensure that their students were exposed to the full range of clients and patients required to fulfil their criteria. It is accepted in traditional examination situations (Nicholas) that assessment will only sample the range of skills but in his preparation Nicholas uses all the assessment methods over a period of time.

Recency is satisfied in that all are current students. If Carol were presented with certification gained more than 5 years ago she might need to carry out a test of her own to check that the knowledge or skill was still current.

Fairness

It is difficult to establish fairness without seeing the actual wording of assessment tasks but you may have noticed certain weaknesses in these case situations.

ACTIVITY | Note any actual or potential unfairness in each of the cases.

Here are some suggestions:

Nicholas
Nicholas himself has behaved fairly but the traditional examination system can be perceived as unfair in several ways:

- you must perform on someone else's chosen date and time;
- the place of assessment is unfamiliar;
- there are strangers as assessors or invigilators;
- the atmosphere may seem threatening, producing nerves;
- sample of knowledge required may favour luck not merit;
- you have to perform against the clock – may not suit adults;
- it favours those who can write well, whatever the subject;
- you cannot check the meaning of the questions;
- no feedback other than grade; if you fail, no guidance on where or how to improve.

In fact this seems like a system designed to catch learners out rather than to encourage them to succeed (Figure 9.1).

◀ **Figure 9.1**
Some forms of assessment
can cause a lot of anxiety.

Carol

The NVQ system prides itself on being fair, provided that you are working in the relevant occupational area to begin with, or, as a student, you can be assessed in a realistic work environment. Carol's work shows the way this approach to assessment avoids unfair discrimination.

All the students are familiar with all the criteria against which they will be assessed and these have been explained to them. The course team has a consistent approach which it has checked with its internal and external verifiers. Each student has an individual assessment plan which is negotiated with them, including their readiness for assessment. Special arrangements are made for people with difficulties. The oral and written questions that will be used are given to the students beforehand. There are no surprises. This is assessment designed to encourage learners to do well. However, Carol must make sure that she does not set unrealistically simple tasks or ask leading questions.

In addition, all students are assessed against the same criteria by a trained assessor whose judgements are checked at two levels. Even the large amount of paperwork which NVQ Level 3 Hairdressing involves, is supposedly there to safeguard the students' interests.

Barbara

The systems Barbara is using are unlikely to discriminate unfairly, unless she shows bias by choosing easier patients for some trainees. Since she is preparing them for someone else to assess this would not help them, and in any case it would be picked up by her supervisor.

Wanda

Wanda's system, with its open checklist and one-to-one attention during practical work, is designed for fairness. She might discriminate unfairly by spending more time with one student than another, by not asking the same questions of everyone, and by variations in her manner of asking (with no one to check on this): but the students do not regard her sessions as offering formal systematic assessment in the first place. For her own support she needs another teacher–assessor with whom to share ideas on giving feedback. She may, without guidance, have misjudged the level implied by Beginners.

You can see from this small sample of teachers that assessment is a huge topic which you have just begun to explore. You will probably want to go on to examine it further, in books and in discussion with your colleagues.

We are now turning our attention to the practical business of designing and implementing assessment instruments and schemes.

Managing the assessment process

As a teacher/trainer you can expect to be asked to create assessment schemes and individual tests, either on your own or as part of a course team or work group. Even if your current role is only to administer existing schemes, you need to understand the full process of design, implementation and evaluation as part of your professional credibility. You may be asked to produce a single test (assessment instrument) and organise its implementation (the assessment event); you may be asked to produce a coherent series of tests for a specific course or group in a particular context (scheme of assessment); you may be asked to contribute ideas to a working party on assessment principles and practice in the organisation (assessment policy). You may, of course, act on your own initiative to promote any one of these activities in your own teaching/learning situation.

The term 'management of the assessment process' implies that you are involved in a series of linked activities directed towards a goal. You are steering the assessment activity through a sequence of stages. This is so whether you are designing a full scheme or a single assessment instrument.

ACTIVITY

Suggest what you think the stages might be.
   Here is a model with eight stages:

(1) Design the scheme overall and the tests which are part of it;
(2) Plan and prepare the implementation of the scheme;
(3) Administer the scheme and tests (gather evidence);
(4) Scrutinise the evidence and make judgements;
(5) Give feedback;
(6) Record the outcomes and process the records;
(7) Evaluate the tests and the scheme overall;
(8) Amend the scheme and tests as needed.

You might find this easier to imagine as a diagram – see Figure 9.2.

Let's now explore each stage in turn. The design stage is the most complex because you are taking many factors into account in order to produce both overview and detailed parts. It is a similar process to producing your programme or scheme of work.

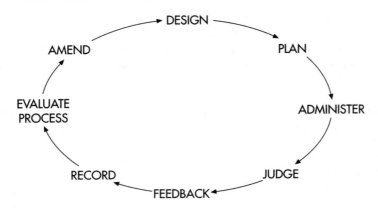

◀ **Figure 9.2**
Managing the assessment
process (courtesy of
Andrew Reeves).

Designing assessment

This is the decision-making stage. Before taking decisions about actual assessment events and sequences you will have to do some research, just as you did before you made your planning decisions. Look back at Chapter 3 *Planning for Learning* to rehearse these areas of investigation.

You will need to check on your own role in assessment, that is, what is expected of you and what you are allowed to do. You will need to check aspects of the learning programme, particularly its level and the type and weighting of the objectives. Check also on when assessment takes place, for example, is it a modular scheme? You will need to be clear about the purpose of assessment on the programme; are you measuring attainment or diagnosing strengths and weaknesses or giving formative feedback? You need to know about the learners/candidates, including how familiar they are with systems of assessment. Finally, you need to consider the costs of various assessment options, including both time and financial costs.

Once you have gathered this information, you will have a framework of opportunities and constraints within which to design your scheme and tests. Now make your design decisions.

Design decisions

These are the key decision areas:

- **What you will assess** – the particular objectives from the scheme of work and as weighted in it.

Imagine you are compiling a Short Answer Test of 10 questions to be answered in 30 minutes on Security of Computerised Information. The objectives require students to be able to apply regulations in a range of circumstances. They first have to learn the regulations, but since application is more important than recall, you could plan your test to have four questions on remembering regulations and six questions on applying the rules in 'what if?' situations. Your mark scheme would reflect the greater importance of these six.

- **Type of test** – you will need to choose types which suit the objectives, such as essays if you need students to reason at length, practicals to demonstrate manual skills. Look back in the first part of this chapter at the range of choices.

- **Type of marking criteria** – will you use pass/fail or grading? Will learners' performance be judged against a norm, against criteria or against their own previous standard? What will your pass mark be? How will you allocate the marks – across the tests or within each test?

- **Amount of testing/number of tests** – how many and how big in the time available, bearing in mind that you need time to teach and develop learning (a good assessment itself might do some of this for you)?

- **Timing of the testing** – how frequently and how spaced out will the testing be, remembering that you will probably need time for test preparation, revision and feedback processes? You will also have to avoid inappropriate times like vacation periods and times which disadvantage some students, such as residential weekends, early mornings.

The actual design can only be done by you because you possess all the information, but you may find it helpful to look back over the Assessment in theory section of this chapter at the concepts of validity and reliability, and then at the case studies which you analysed in this context.

ACTIVITY | This activity is in two parts. First look at an assessment test which you have devised. How effective do you think it will be? Make yourself a checklist of criteria it should fulfil, based on the ideas in this chapter. Then repeat this process to produce a checklist of effectiveness for a complete scheme of assessment. You can put these to use later in the chapter.

Checklist of characteristics of an effective test

Does my test?

- discriminate clearly between those who do know the answers and those who do not;
- do this whenever used and no matter who marks it;
- test what it sets out to test;
- relate clearly to the learning objectives;
- demonstrate to the students that it relates to their learning objectives;
- take an appropriate form to suit the objectives, for example, practical test for skills, objective test for recall;
- have clearly expressed criteria on whose meaning assessors and students are agreed;
- have clearly expressed instructions to follow;
- cover a sensible amount of material;
- avoid personal discrimination against any candidate;
- contain interesting material or challenges to motivate students and help their learning;
- take a reasonable time to assess;
- avoid excessive paperwork.

Checklist of characteristics of an effective scheme of assessment

Does my scheme?

- provide variety in the types of test used, to maintain learners' interest and to suit all learners;
- use only valid and reliable tests;
- avoid putting any learner at a disadvantage;
- communicate its requirements clearly to learners and assessors;
- suit the nature of the learning group;
- match the aims and objectives of the learning;
- use straightforward administration procedures;
- allow time for preparation and feedback;
- avoid dominating the time for learning;
- use assessment tasks which promote learning as well as testing;
- have deadlines which are sufficiently flexible to avoid causing learners hardship;
- avoid excessive paperwork;
- operate without heavy time demands on assessors and verifiers;
- operate within a reasonable budget.

If your design decisions fulfil these criteria, you are ready for the next stage in the cycle.

Planning and preparing for assessment

Let's move on to the practicalities of getting your assessment ideas and materials into use. This stage is about implementation. It includes a good many small administrative tasks which are not exciting but, if omitted or muddled, will lead to complete chaos and destroy your credibility very quickly. Assessment, like teaching, is at least 50% organisation. No one wants assessment to go wrong, least of all the candidates.

Essentially you are making all the arrangements for the smooth running of the assessment events. A large part of this involves communication. Key people who need to know about your intentions include students, other members of your course or programme team, if you have them, internal verifiers and moderators and line managers.

You may also need to communicate with:

- Technicians for provision of materials and equipment;
- Reprographics to get papers copied in good time;
- Caretakers to get venues booked and set up, and clocks provided;
- Those responsible for the secure storage of papers before and after a test;
- The post room if material is to be sent outside;
- Invigilators, who will need thorough briefing.

Preparing students

You will need to communicate your assessment decisions to your students at several levels and on many occasions. These could include at interview, at induction, when action planning, before each assessment event, and, indeed, whenever they ask. You will need to explain the overall assessment system (for example, GNVQs) and the

particular scheme for their situation (Figure 9.3). This will include the approach to marking and grading. They will want details of each task, its criteria and procedures.

For some of you 'explain' may mean 'tell' while for others it may mean 'negotiate'. It should always include answering queries, even if they seem to you to have been answered before. It is not you whose achievement is being judged.

It is particularly important to ensure that candidates understand the rubric, the instructions about what they should and should not do, which in formal exams is read out before the event. It is well worth checking any written briefing material with a colleague at this stage to see if it is as unambiguous as you supposed.

> **ACTIVITY**
>
> Now that you have completed your planning, compile another checklist, this time of the characteristics of an effective assessment event.

A checklist of characteristics of an effective assessment event

- everyone involved is informed in good time;
- administrative details are carried out smoothly;
- learners are well prepared for the event;
- if the assessment is in the workplace, it does not interfere with normal work;
- regulations are followed strictly to ensure fairness for all students;
- security is maintained in relation to scripts and assessment materials;
- staff administering the assessment are calm and pleasant.

You have now covered two of the eight stages but you have covered at least 50% of the work involved. These first two stages form the bedrock of successful assessment, though of course all stages are important.

Administering assessment events

Now run the events as they have been planned – and respond intelligently to unexpected crises.

Scrutinising evidence to make judgements

At this stage you may be with the candidates, for example if you are assessing by observation of activities, or you may be looking through portfolios, test papers, essays, or looking at items produced for assessment – hair styled, equipment assembled, a set of dress patterns or a display of advertising leaflets. In all cases you will be using your assessment checklist or mark sheet to match what you are seeing (or hearing, tasting, smelling, touching) with the desired criteria.

Between this stage and the next (giving feedback) you may have to do some other checking, perhaps on the authenticity of written work. You may be unsure whether the form in which evidence has been presented is allowable, and want to check with a more experienced colleague. You may find that a candidate has an alternative interpretation of criteria which you want to clear with your internal verifier. You may, in fact, have a formal meeting set up at which several of you who are assessing, say, a written paper or a set of designs or a video submission, meet to discuss sample items to standardise, that is, agree, the level of your judgements before marking the rest of the submissions.

We all improve our skill in making judgements with practice, but it is always a situation where you are anxious in case you make mistakes. If you are in any doubt, consult a colleague rather than floundering on your own. No one will think less of you for being unsure. Checklists of criteria and mark schemes help to reduce ambiguity but, except for multichoice objective tests, there can still be a range of interpretation of criteria. You should double check your decisions and be able to justify the basis on which you made them, but if doubt remains it is more professional to delay a decision while you consult, than to go it alone. Most teachers who are assessing are part of a system, and there will be supervisors or verifiers to whom you can refer.

At this stage your greatest strength is the assessment checklist you created when you devised your tests, or the one you have been given and had yourself briefed to use. With this, and helpful colleagues, you can cope with doubts and challenges. If a candidate or student challenges you at the feedback stage, you can help them to make use of the organisation's appeals policy if they don't accept your justification. All centres offering NVQs and GNVQs must have such an appeals policy, and nowadays most places offering assessment services will have one.

Giving feedback to candidates

You have already thought about the content and manner of giving feedback as part of formative assessment while teaching or in tutorials while reviewing progress. Look back at Chapter 7 *Teaching a Skill* and Chapter 8 *Supporting the Individual Learner* if you want to refresh your memory of these processes. Let's concentrate now on giving feedback as part of the assessment event.

Many of you will be able to give your students individual feedback immediately or very soon after their assessment events. This will be in the form of verbal commentary, sets of marks, brief written summaries or combinations of these. Sometimes a mark can speak for itself in a simple test, but marks alone, unaccompanied by some words from the teacher, are a poor sort of feedback. The student has the result; this is not the same as having feedback. The latter term implies some degree of detail on strengths and weaknesses, accompanied by words of praise and encouragement. The purpose of feedback is to help learners learn and improve; they want to know what to do next *after* the result.

If you look back at the case studies you examined earlier, you can see that some of the students who are best served, are those who are given individual feedback on their development session by session, as in the class taken by Wanda.

By comparison Nicholas' students, as candidates in a traditional external examination, will have little but a mark or grade to go on. This is why it is so important for teachers in his position to use mock exams and tests, so that they can give students the feedback they need to guide their development.

All feedback, whether in practice sessions or in assessment events, should be **specific, positive, accurate** and **recorded**.

If you are giving written feedback you need to choose the words carefully. That which is written has greater status than that which is spoken, and can be a source of delight, puzzlement or anguish. It is essential to be clear and unambiguous. It is helpful to be positive about future steps and optimistic about improvements. It is not helpful to try to be kind and dress up your sympathy for a student's disappointment in expressions which obscure the poor nature of the work. Be positive, but be accurate and truthful first.

Recording assessment outcomes and processing records

This is a necessary and straightforward process. Never trust to memory alone. It is vital that every candidate gets their correct result, even if the paperwork is time consuming. It is equally important if you are giving formative feedback in a non-assessed course to have a record of how each student has done. If all the progress information is in your head the students are at a disadvantage. You might be unable to continue with their class for various reasons, leaving the next teacher with no guidance. In any situation, there might be a dispute over the assessment decision, the teaching team may change or a student may want the information for accreditation on another programme or need a reference. Overall you should aim for records that are complete, accurate, given in by the deadline and, of course, legible.

Processing the records

At this stage you are storing or passing on information about your students' achievements. There will be regulations to follow, unless you are devising and implementing your own scheme. If you are assessing NVQs or GNVQs you will have made arrangements with your internal verifier for sampling and checking to be carried out. This is a fairly tidy process if the whole cohort is presenting at once. You will need to be well organised to deal with the paperwork and storage of evidence if it comes in unit by unit from separate candidates. This is when your paper or computer record needs to be updated regularly.

Maintaining confidentiality and security by storing records in secure locations is also an important responsibility. This may sound dull, but once you have experienced the heart-stopping moment of losing a candidate's coursework or a sheet of the table of results, you will appreciate the necessity.

You will need to pass a copy of the assessment records to other involved people, your internal verifier, members of the course team, a line manager and possibly an examinations officer for your organisation/workplace. It may be your responsibility to inform the learners of their results. It might be worth setting up a system for this, such as an appropriately worded standard letter or form which you can process quickly.

In summary, for this stage, check that you have:

- passed the assessment records on to the next stage in their processing, such as the examinations officer or internal verifier;
- passed the assessment data to anyone else who needs to know, such as the line manager or course team;
- informed the candidates, if it is your role to do so (you would have to wait until the internal verifier and/or external representative from the awarding body had confirmed your judgements);
- stored the records and any other materials securely or ensured that another responsible person is doing so;
- **kept a copy of every essential record in a secure place.**

Evaluating assessment tests and schemes

You will need to examine three aspects of your assessment activities:

- the results of the test or tests;
- your students' feedback about the test(s) and the assessment process;
- feedback from anyone else involved, such as the course team, external and internal verifiers and possibly employers of the students who have invested in their learning.

This can be quite a complex process, so set aside time for it.

How could you go about collecting feedback on your assessment activities? There are several possibilities:

- use the checklists you invented earlier for judging the effectiveness of tests, events and schemes of assessment – you could turn them into a questionnaire to give to candidates;
- have a verbal debrief with a group or representatives of it gathered for the purpose, and record their points;
- have a course team meeting using the external verifier's report (and the students' feedback);
- set up a meeting of interested employers to discuss your methods of assessment and to hear their views;
- invite a critical friend who assesses in another subject area to discuss your findings with you.

Amending assessment decisions

The final stage of the cycle is to use the feedback from your evaluation to review your original design decisions. Then make changes to your scheme, to individual tests or to the organisation of assessment events, as required. It is best to consult your colleagues about the changes you intend to make, in case there are implications which you have not foreseen.

Summary

You have now examined assessment in theory and assessment in practice. You have explored key concepts in assessment, particularly validity and reliability. You have worked your way through the stages necessary to manage the assessment process, seeing its significance both for formal and less formal assessment situations.

We are now approaching the final stage of the teaching/training cycle, that of evaluation. In evaluation, as in planning, you revisit each stage of your decision making and action. Your review of your findings from evaluation will then lead you to move forward again round the cycle with fresh ideas for implementation.

10 Evaluation

All teachers and trainers evaluate their work to some degree; many do so regularly and systematically. They monitor their lessons in progress and look back on them when they are completed. They review whole courses and learning programmes in consultation with colleagues and learners. They discuss their current professional competence and their future development needs with their line managers. They do these things because they are committed, on the one hand, to providing better learning opportunities for their students, and, on the other hand, to managing their own long-term development.

In this chapter you are going to explore what is meant by evaluation and your role in it. You will look at ways of monitoring and reviewing your own progress, particularly in your teaching. You will examine in detail procedures for evaluating both individual sessions and complete courses and learning programmes, and at the action planning which follows.

You will look in particular at established procedures which will enable you to evaluate your work systematically.

Systematic evaluation

We are going to look at ways of managing the process of evaluation which require a fully organised approach.

Systematic evaluation has the following characteristics:

- it is undertaken for a particular purpose;
- it implies a commitment to act on the results, that is, to change;
- it occurs at regular, pre-set intervals;
- it uses sets of criteria against which to make judgements;
- it involves a range of people;
- it gathers data from several sources;
- it combines 'hard' (facts and figures) and 'soft' (feelings) data (also called quantitative and qualitative data);
- it uses accepted formats to organise data gathering and reporting;
- it results in an action plan with realistic objectives and timescales and allocated responsibilities for change;
- it sets target dates for reviewing the effect of the changes.

Professionally conducted evaluation always:

- respects confidentiality in the collection and dissemination of data;
- gives full acknowledgement to positive findings before suggesting areas for development.

Initial considerations

The purpose of evaluation

Evaluation is the process of finding out how close you have come to achieving your goals. It is closely linked to assessment. You have to know how well your students have done (assessment) before you can ask the question 'How well have I done?' (evaluation).

You may be asking these questions for a variety of reasons. You may be motivated by your own concern for high standards. You may be part of a team which is committed to examining its course against particular criteria, for example, monitoring for equal opportunities. You may be required by your workplace to carry out evaluation as part of its quality assurance processes.

There is often a wider dimension to evaluation, which links it to economic and political considerations. Within the state system of further education, colleges are required to evaluate their provision against criteria set by the body which funds them on behalf of the government. They collect statistics relating to student enrolment, retention and achievement rates. Poor performance can result in loss of funding as well as disappointed learners. A thorough evaluation may be carried out to discover the cause of the problem.

Since all colleges want to attract students, they also collect 'soft' data from students – what did they like about their courses which motivated them to stay, and do they have suggestions for improvements?

In the private sector, effective training can help businesses stay in business and fight off the competition. Trainers naturally want to know what makes their programmes acceptable to trainees and what effect the training has on later work practice.

Before you embark on any evaluation, find out or decide whether its purpose is to:

- improve the learning process for the **current** students;
- improve the learning process for **future** students;
- provide data to judge your own effectiveness;
- provide data to estimate the value of the programme to the workplace or to another agency, such as employers;
- assist in making decisions about the continuing viability of the programme.

In fact, there are three related questions you can ask:

> What is the purpose of the evaluation?
> Who requires the information generated by the evaluation?
> What will they do with the information?

These three questions have a bearing on what you evaluate and whom you consult, what you ask and how you present the results. You need to think carefully about issues of confidentiality, particularly for those who give soft data. An evaluation report can be a powerful document and should be treated with respect.

Your role in the wider context

Nowadays evaluation takes place in a context of rapid change. Virtually every aspect of the world of education and training for people over the age of 16 is undergoing development. The government-backed introduction of competence-based qualifications (NVQs and GNVQs) has had effects on assessment practices, on the way courses are structured and taught, and on qualifications for teachers and trainers. Changes in the governing and funding of colleges have led to many organisational developments. New groups of learners are being attracted to further education. New learning tools are being developed through computer technology, and the material to be learned requires constant updating as technologies also change.

You can expect to be asked to take on a number of new roles. These might include (see Figure 10.1):

- programme or course leader
- budget holder
- liaison tutor – external agencies
- marketing representative
- personal tutor
- internal verifier

You may be asked to develop skills in producing high-quality computer-generated teaching and learning materials, to work with very large class numbers, to devise courses for unfamiliar groups of students, to train workers in operating new equipment, to introduce NVQs in the workplace or to coordinate a training programme in different offices spread over a large area. In this context it is in your own professional interests to evaluate your continuing effectiveness and to plan for your own development as well as that of your students.

Choosing what you will evaluate

However, when it comes to evaluation, yours is a many-sided role. You will need to select from the totality of your professional practice those aspects on which you will

◄ **Figure 10.1**
Teachers need to be
flexible.

focus. It is always more effective to concentrate on one or two parts of your role than to skim over the surface of everything.

Both assessment and evaluation use the concept of sampling. When you were assessing, you chose certain aspects of knowledge, understanding, skill and attitude to test, which gave you a valid picture of each student's capacities. Similarly in evaluating your own capacities you can sample your activities. It is most likely that you will want to evaluate your teaching, rather than your other duties.

As you have worked through the chapters of this book you have investigated your own role in getting to know your students' needs, planning for their learning, using a range of teaching and learning strategies, aids and resources, monitoring your students' progress and assessing their achievements. You are now in a good position to choose one of those key stages to evaluate, such as your planning skills or your grasp of assessment processes.

Alternatively, you could use the overview of teaching you have gained to look closely at your lessons/sessions with one or two particular types of group or learner. You could choose two classes and compare your effectiveness with each of them. You could compare your management of older learners with that of a young adult group.

The choice is yours. In the next section you will be introduced to a systematic approach to evaluating individual sessions.

Evaluating individual sessions and lessons

You are going to ask the question, 'How effective was this session in helping my students or trainees learn effectively?'

Knowing what you want to achieve

Before you can measure how well a process has created an effect, you need to have a picture of what the desired good practice would look like in the first place. You need to specify the targets or standards that you are aiming to meet. What are the criteria which you are measuring your lesson or session against?

These criteria may be those which you have devised yourself, or, more likely, they will be standards set by your workplace, an awarding body (like City & Guilds or BTEC), or a national body like NCVQ. You will have investigated these when you were planning your learning programmes and schemes of assessment.

ACTIVITY | Imagine a colleague is going to sit in on one of your lessons to give you feedback on its effectiveness in promoting your students' learning. Discuss with your colleague the characteristics which you think all lessons should have to make them effective. Draw up this list of criteria.

Here are some suggestions which relate to lessons in general. All lessons should:

- Have clear objectives
- Engage all students actively in learning
- Provide evidence of learning/assess learning
- Be structured
- Provide a safe and healthy learning environment
- Enable all learners to feel valued
- Build on prior learning
- Go at a suitable pace
- Hit the right level of understanding
- Fit into the time available
- Use suitable learning strategies
- Use resources appropriately
- Motivate students to go on learning

Now go on to draw up criteria for the particular lesson/session which you will arrange for your colleague to observe. You could set this out as a 'Did I?' checklist. (Look back at Chapter 3 *Planning for Learning* to remind yourself of this.) If you work as part of a team you may want to devise a common set of criteria to which you could all work.

Collecting your data

There are three ways you can go about this – you can consult the facts, consult your own judgement or consult the judgement of others. In this case, the facts are the results of learning, the assessment results; the others are either the learners or your colleagues, or both. Each approach on its own is limited and will only give you part of the story.

 Identify the limitations of each approach.

Here are some suggestions:

(1) Checking the results
  - students may achieve in spite of poor teaching;
  - good teaching may be lost at assessment time if students are nervous, ill-prepared or distracted by personal problems.

(2) Asking students and colleagues
  - students may not feel they can be honest, especially if you are assessing their work;
  - students cannot always see or appreciate the wider context into which a lesson fits;

- students may vote for easy options and against challenging approaches which promote greater learning in the long run;
- colleagues may feel constrained to be polite;
- colleagues may have fixed styles of their own which they try to impose on you;
- colleagues may not appreciate fully the dynamic of your group;
- colleagues may know the material already, so cannot appreciate the learners' position.

(3) Consulting your own judgement
   - it is difficult to be objective about our own efforts;
   - we tend to be more negative than positive about our own work;
   - we are so bound up in the lesson that we are likely to miss quite a lot of significant points;
   - thorough self-evaluation is hard work, and difficult to fit in to a busy schedule; we tend to accept immediate impressions and miss out fuller reflection.

Ideally, then, you need to use several approaches: to monitor the students' progress, to consult students about their feelings on the way the sessions are run, to consult your colleagues for feedback on the aspects you and the students may have missed, and to use your own judgement to create an overall picture.

Evaluation forms and formats

The materials which you use for gathering evidence about your effectiveness and that of your lessons are sometimes called evaluation **instruments** (just as assessment materials are called assessment instruments); this simply means that they are the tools with which you do the job. There are many different tools, and you will need to choose the ones you judge most appropriate for the situation and the people involved.

Let's look now at a range of possible tools through the eyes of a group of teachers and trainers who are involved in monitoring the effectiveness of their lessons. Later you can see what kind of feedback they gained, and what action plans they drew up to respond to the feedback. We'll begin with Suzanne, since her approach is one you could use regularly for your own sessions.

Suzanne is a trainer with a large retail company. She is about to run a series of sessions on customer care for point-of-sales staff from several retail outlets in the chain. She will give the participants a monitoring form after each session, using a rating scale to make it easy for them to record their responses. She will monitor her own performance by using two evaluation formats, one for immediate impressions, one for later reflection. She hopes these three formats together will give her useful feedback on which to base future sessions. You can see her evaluation instruments (formats) reproduced in Figure 10.2 on pages 156 to 158.

IMMEDIATE IMPRESSIONS		
Date Group Session title Key session objectives		
	POSITIVE POINTS	LESS POSITIVE POINTS
ME		
THEM		
ROOM/ RESOURCES		

▲ **Figure 10.2**
Make a note of immediate
impressions (continued on
pages 157 and 158).

```
┌────────────────────────────────────────────────────────────┐
│                      ON REFLECTION                         │
│                                                            │
│   Date                          Group                      │
│   Session title                                            │
│   Key session objectives                                   │
├────────────────────────────────────────────────────────────┤
│   Structure of session                                     │
│                                                            │
│                                                            │
│   Relevance of material                                    │
│                                                            │
│                                                            │
│   Level                                                    │
│                                                            │
│                                                            │
│   Timing and pacing                                        │
│                                                            │
│                                                            │
│   Teaching and learning strategies                         │
│                                                            │
│                                                            │
│   Venue and resources                                      │
│                                                            │
│                                                            │
│   Relationships with students                              │
│                                                            │
│                                                            │
│   ASPECTS TO WORK ON                                       │
└────────────────────────────────────────────────────────────┘
```

▲ **Figure 10.2** (continued)

SESSION MONITORING FORM

Date
Session title

Please answer the questions below by circling the appropriate number. This will help me to review the session. Thank you.

1. To what extent do you think the session objectives were met?
   LOW   HIGH
   1   2   3   4   5   6

2. To what extent was the material relevant to you?
   LOW   HIGH
   1   2   3   4   5   6

3. How useful do you think the material will be in your work?
   LOW   HIGH
   1   2   3   4   5   6

4. How satisfied were you with the session activities?
   LOW   HIGH
   1   2   3   4   5   6

5. How satisfied were you with the learning environment?
   LOW   HIGH
   1   2   3   4   5   6

Please continue overleaf if you have any comments you would like to make.

▲ Figure 10.2 (continued)

Stephen, the second teacher in this group, is teaching Basic Programming to a group of students in a private college, for most of whom English is not their first language. He has tried asking the students if his approach is suitable for them but they are very reluctant to comment. So he has invented a very simple questionnaire which can be completed anonymously after each lesson or at intervals.

> **Please help me to get the sessions right for you.**
> **Please complete the following sentences according to how you feel. Thank you.**
>
> It helps me when you ....
> ....
>
> It is difficult for me when you ....
> ....
>
> I would like more ....
> ....
>
> I would like less ....
> ....

Loretta, teaching Women's Institute members the skills of chairing meetings, has adopted the method of the round. She feels this is suitable for a group of mature people with a high degree of trust. Her group sits in a circle, or round, at the end of the session. Each takes it in turn to make one positive statement about the session. No one discusses anyone's points. Anyone who does not want to make a statement can say 'Pass'. After this round is complete, speakers go round again making negative points. Each week a different member of the group sits out to note down the points for Loretta to take away and think about later.

Loretta thinks this strategy is valuable because it makes individuals take responsibility for their own views, it gives the whole group an idea of what everyone is feeling, and it gets views out in the open. There is a certain amount of group pressure for everyone to contribute. The group members have said they like the method, now they have got used to it, especially as it does not involve any writing.

Leo has a group of mature students who are on a return to study course. This group are shy of speaking out individually. Leo has two ways of dealing with this when it comes to evaluation. The first is to adopt the 1/2/4/8 method, also called snowballing because of the way contributions build up. Students are invited to make three positive points about the session, or course, and then three negative points.

They do this first of all on their own, then in pairs, then in 4s by combining two pairs, and finally in 8s by combining two 4s. By this time all the points have been discussed fully and any individual feels they have the support of their sub-group in making their points. Leo realises that some less vehemently argued points may get lost along the way, but feels enough should be left to give the flavour of the group's opinions.

Leo's other technique is to pin two large sheets of flip chart paper on the wall, one headed 'Positive points', the other headed 'Points to work on', then to leave the room so that students can write up their comments anonymously. The sheets can then be taken away for later consideration.

Michael teaches medical personnel within the prison service. His unit has a policy of evaluating their teaching. He has decided to use a critical incident log over a 6-

week period. His aim is to pick out two events each week which are significant **to him** because they have made him think about his teaching. He will keep a record of the events, his feelings about them and what he feels he has learned. He has devised the following proforma to help himself do the analysis systematically.

CRITICAL INCIDENT LOG

Date   Group
Lesson topic

Any significant differences from usual practice, for example, different venue, number or composition of the group, duration of session

Critical incident (brief description)

Why I think the incident is significant

What I have learned from the incident

What I need to do as a result of this learning

Tina has taken her students into her confidence about her need to analyse their hair-dressing practical sessions which are proving disorganised. They are busy sessions with several outside models who are often late for appointments. Within the session Tina is too busy coping with minor crises to keep an eye on everyone. She has decided, with the students' permission, to ask a colleague with a small camcorder to video the next two sessions. Later Tina will watch the video to see what she can learn. Her students are quite blasé about the camera, they are used to modelling, mirrors and being on show.

Finally, Bill. He is keen to develop his skills in using discussion with his evening accounts class. They are all mature students with accounting duties in their daytime jobs, so should have plenty to say. He wants detailed feedback so has asked a more experienced teacher of the same subject, Hari, to sit in on the session. It is not unusual for Bill to have observers in his sessions, usually student teachers picking up tips, so the class is unlikely to be put off.

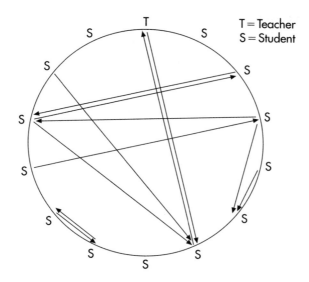

◀ **Figure 10.3**
Patterns of interaction
quickly become apparent.

Hari is going to make notes against a checklist which she and Bill have devised, and draw an interaction analysis chart. This is a diagram based on a seating plan, on which Hari draws lines representing who speaks to whom during two 10-minute slices of the lesson. Bill can then study the pattern of interaction.

The chart is built up like the one shown in Figure 10.3.

The checklist points which Hari will note are:

● Objectives clearly communicated   ....

● Purpose of activity explained   ....

● Discussion method described   ....

● Questions on method invited   ....

● Topic introduced   ....

● Contributions prompted   ....

● Relevance explained   ....

● All class included   ....

● Pacing appropriate   ....

● Learning summarised   ....

ACTIVITY

Now imagine yourself in a situation where you would like to gather feedback on your teaching. Choose one of the case study approaches or devise one of your own. Think through each of the stages, including creating a checklist if you think it would be useful. Discuss your ideas with a colleague if possible.

Looking at your findings

Now let's look at the feedback the group of teachers received from their students, colleagues and technological aids.

You gather feedback in order to learn from it. It may reveal that all is well, confirming the decisions which you had made and the actions which you had taken. It may reveal some areas for development, or for minor adjustment, which you can incorporate into your next lesson or next planning cycle. It may reveal the need for a major rethink.

Never respond instantly to feedback, either to become defensive or to leap into action. First review the context in which the feedback was given – by whom, to whom, when in the programme, at whose invitation and so on. Don't pick out the one negative point in a wealth of positives and treat it as a disaster.

Suzanne, teaching customer relations, was not very satisfied with her performance. She noted her immediate impressions as follows.

	POSITIVE POINTS	LESS POSITIVE POINTS
Me	Well prepared Enthusiastic Good overheads	Talked too much Stuck behind desk Moralising tone
Them	Well behaved Plenty of experience	Most not joining in One dominated with anecdotes
Room/ Resources	Private, quiet Training aids good	Very formal furniture fixed in position

This initial feeling that the session had failed to take off and had been hijacked by the one person who did contribute, was confirmed in Suzanne's later analysis after reflection. She felt that she had been so grateful for contributions that she had failed to control 'the talker'. She is going to have to create more interaction involving the whole group – maybe a different room with movable furniture?

The feedback from the ratings sheets filled in by the learners showed mainly 4s, a group playing safe, except for one person brave enough to write on the back of the sheet

'Can't we do some role play?'

Suzanne felt she had enough here to work on changes for the next session.

Stephen, teaching computer programming, was delighted with the response to his low key form. It had inspired the shy students to venture their views. He got back:

1. It helps me when
   – you speak slowly
   – you help us individually
   – you put things on the board

2. It is difficult when
   – you dictate notes
   – you talk for a long time non-stop

3. I would like more
   – personal attention
   – handouts

4. I would like less
   – dictation

Loretta's trainee chairwomen spoke in favour of sitting so that they could all see each other, the informative handouts and the 10-minute break when they could share ideas informally. They wanted an opportunity to practise the skills she demonstrated so well, and advice on problem situations. Loretta could see at once where the sessions needed to go.

Michael, teaching anatomy and physiology, has one very significant entry in his critical incident log. This is the poor results his students achieved on their mid-course test for all the questions in the application of knowledge section. They did well on the multiple-choice factual recall section. This suggested that they had learned parrot fashion, but could not apply the facts because they did not understand their significance. His formal transmission style of teaching with too little questioning is clearly to blame.

Tina is feeling very positive because she can see from the video why her hairdressing practical classes are so stressful. Clients are arriving late and being slotted in with the nearest stylist. Students who are hiding cannily behind mirrors or in the stockroom are not doing their share of the work and can be idle for long periods. She herself is trying to keep all the clients happy rather than managing the students. Clearly she needs a system.

Bill is cross with himself for making a couple of basic mistakes and almost overlooks the wealth of positive feedback which Hari gives him about his discussion session with his accounts class. He can see from her interaction analysis chart that three people have not taken part. Two of them are the individuals on his immediate right and left in the circle, with whom he cannot make eye contact.

Others are reluctant to make eye contact with them in case they catch the tutor's eye instead. The third person is the one immediately opposite Bill who has resolutely withheld eye contact throughout. Bill has come to the unhappy conclusion that this student finds him intimidating. What shall he do about this?

Devising a plan of action

The next stage after you have gathered and reviewed the feedback on your sessions is to identify solutions to the problems. Then you draw up an action plan for putting your solutions into practice. The logic and imagination needed to perceive the next steps are qualities which develop with experience. The courage to put them into operation is another matter. Most of us have the wit to perceive when we need to change, and to work out what it is that we need to do. Drawing up an action plan is an essential preliminary step to action but it will not guarantee it. You still need to find the will to adopt a different method of communication, to confront the challenge of new technology, to try different teaching strategies, to update your subject skills, to take whatever you have identified as the next step.

Suzanne, Stephen and their colleagues are now at the action planning stage.

ACTIVITY

Draw up an action plan for one of the teachers in the case studies. You could discuss your ideas with a colleague. This example uses a format which you might find helpful.

Tina's action plan

Aims of the action
1. to keep all students engaged continuously in learning tasks;
2. to share the workload fairly;
3. to keep track of what everyone is doing.

Proposals

Long-term
Develop a systematic approach to practical sessions which students come to expect.

Short-term
(1) Make a list of tasks for the session and allocate them to students: students come to me when task is completed, I check their work and give them a new task.
(2) Devise tasks students can do while waiting for models.
(3) Models arriving late must wait for an appropriate student to suit work rota.

Help needed: none.

Suzanne wants to increase her trainees' interaction in the session and to draw on their experience. She plans in the long term to develop a more interactive style of teaching. In the short term she will change her room to one with flexible furniture which she can arrange into a U-shape. She will vary her presentations with case studies, simulation and role play.

Stephen aims to increase his students' understanding of the technical material. He will try to boost their learning rate by giving them more individual attention. Eventually he would like to develop some open learning material for them to use at their own pace. For the moment he will produce some work sheets; the students can use these while he circulates to monitor their work. He will also try to speak more slowly and distinctly.

Loretta is all set to use role play and case studies so that her students can practise the skills she has demonstrated. In future she will consult students early in the course about their preferred styles of learning, and be prepared to adjust her teaching scheme. She will also aim to get a video set up so that they can record and evaluate their own developing skills.

Michael is going to develop questioning techniques to help his students apply their learning. He will break up the factual material with periods for questions, and use visual aids to consolidate his points. He intends to go on a course himself to develop a more interactive style of teaching.

Bill wants to involve his students in discussion without pressuring them. He is going to investigate discussion techniques which do not make participants feel exposed. For the moment he plans to rearrange the seating so that the class sits behind their desks round three sides of a U-shape. He will sit in the gap where he can see everyone comfortably. In front of him he will have a private note telling him 'Don't stare'.

Implementing and reviewing your action plan

Before you start on the implementation of your action plan, you will find it helpful to set a date(s) by which you will review your progress. This gives you a target to aim for. It might be helpful to do this with a colleague, so that you can celebrate together or keep each other up to the mark. Until you have been through this process once it is difficult to judge the feasibility of timescales. There is a temptation to feel you must become a perfect teacher immediately, then to become discouraged. It is better to set yourself a series of achievable steps (as you would do with your students).

There are three important aspects of implementation; they are commitment, communication and timing. Let's look at these briefly, before moving on to examine the process of evaluating course and learning programmes.

Commitment

As you will have noticed, professional development demands considerable commitment. You are exposing yourself in admitting the need for change and in taking risks with unfamiliar approaches. You will be committing time and you may be committing money if you decide that you need further professional or academic development. The rewards will be your own sense of achievement and the greater achievements of the students. It does not matter how small the change is.

Communication

It is easy to overlook the other people who may be implicated in the changes you make. If you decide to move furniture around it is only courteous to consult the caretakers. Similarly you would want to consult the library staff if your students are going to make increased use of their open access areas.

You might also need to talk to your team, if you have one, or to other teachers working with these students. **You** may have decided to introduce discovery methods for very good reasons, but they could come into conflict with the methods used by your colleagues. This could cause the students considerable confusion, as well as undermining your colleagues' lessons. In any case, you should *always* explain to learners why you are introducing a particular approach. They need to be assured that it will help them meet their objectives. Otherwise you will create anxiety which will block the very learning which you wanted to liberate. Invest a little time in explaining the purpose of the new approach, stressing how it will help them, and describing their new roles as learners.

Timing

Think carefully about when to introduce the changes. It is tempting when you have had a sudden revelation to want to carry everyone else along with you at once. This is seldom wise. Students take time to learn the ground rules of particular subjects and teachers. It is unfair to unsettle them suddenly or at certain times when their confidence is low, such as about a third of the way into a course when the initial excitement has worn off and the mountain of learning begins to look impossible, or just before any kind of assessment. Some of your changes may need a long lead time, for instance if you are planning to introduce flexible learning. You may need to induct your students to the method over a period of weeks rather than days.

The timing of the review of your action plan is also important. Give the changes time to work before you look for the effects. Both you and the students will need time to adjust before benefits become apparent.

Evaluating courses and programmes

Much of what has been explored in the previous sections of this chapter applies to the evaluation of courses and learning programmes, but on a larger scale.

Deciding on the focus of your evaluation

Nowadays many teachers and trainers are involved to some degree in monitoring the effectiveness of the programmes on which they work, if only in noting how many students join, how many stay to the end, why the ones who leave do so, and how many achieve the goals they set out to meet. You may be asked to make this kind of report at the end of your course, including qualitative (soft) data on the students' feelings about their learning experiences.

If you are a course or programme manager you may be asked to work out with your course team what the course costs to run, and justify this expenditure in terms of the benefits gained from it by the students directly, and by your place of work indirectly. The benefits gained by students are not just qualifications. There are also gains such as increased social and life skills, and the possibility of progressing to other forms of education.

There are two different perspectives here. One asks if the course is successful in its own right, judged by the teachers/trainers. The other asks whether the course, whatever its degree of success, can justify the expenditure on it – is it worth running in financial terms – judged by managers and budget holders?

The teachers will ask such questions as:

> Is the course/programme meeting its aims?
> Are the students learning?
> Do the students like it?
> Are the organisational arrangements working?

The budget holders ask such questions as:

> How much does it cost to run?
> Can we afford it?
> What do we gain because we run it?
> What would we lose if we didn't run it?

There are two other groups of people concerned in evaluation and they too have questions to ask. One group is the representatives of the professional bodies who award the qualifications, such as City & Guilds and the universities. These external verifiers, moderators and examiners will ask:

> How many students are passing?
> Are the staff properly qualified?
> Do the staff observe all the regulations and procedures laid down by the awarding body correctly?

Then there may be employers who have funded their staff to go to college or who release them for training within the workplace. They want to know if the programmes are meeting employment needs. Employers may ask:

> Are my staff gaining new skills?
> Will they be able to apply what they have learned in the job?
> Have they been motivated to develop themselves further?
> Has it been worth what it has cost me to pay their wages, their fees and to bear the cost of their time off work?

At the heart of all these overlapping perspectives are the views of the learners. These are likely to be the main focus of your evaluation. The learners might ask:

> Was the course/programme well taught and organised?
> Has it prepared us for work/leisure/society/further study?
> Has it been value for the time, money and other opportunities which we gave up to do it?

It is useful to be aware of the wider context of course and programme evaluation when you are deciding on your own focus.

Implementing the procedures

The procedure to follow in evaluating a course or programme of learning is made up of the same steps as when you are evaluating sessions or lessons:

> Decide on the purpose of the evaluation
> Decide what you will evaluate
> Clarify your targets and standards
> Decide how you will gather the data
> Prepare people and materials
> Gather the data
> Review the data
> Identify areas for change and development
> Draw up an action plan
> Report to others if required
> Implement the action plan
> Review the effectiveness of the action plan

This may seem a daunting prospect, but you have already done a great deal of the work. When you planned your course you had a vision of what you wanted it to achieve and the standards you wanted to meet. This gives you your criteria against which to evaluate it, for example, is it accessible to all students?, is it logically structured?, are the activities varied? Look back at Chapter 3 *Planning for Learning* and you will realise how much of the groundwork for evaluation you have covered already.

ACTIVITY

Decide how you are going to collect evaluation data from your students/trainees.

Here are some suggestions:

- give the learners a questionnaire, either the rating scale or open question variety;
- use a snowball discussion technique;
- ask the students directly for positive and negative points which you record, for example, on flip chart paper;
- ask representative students from the group to survey their peers and give you a summary of their views.

If you wanted a livelier approach, you could set up a role play which you video, in which students pretend to be advising prospective recruits about what the course holds in store.

Using a questionnaire

This is the most common evaluation instrument. It need not be an awesome document. The example which follows could be used mid-way through the programme, or at the end, and need only take 20 minutes – or it could lead to 2 hours' discussion.

ACTIVITY

When you have studied the example, draw up your own form.

EVALUATION QUESTIONNAIRE

Title of your course or programme

....

Title of your class or group

....

We are keen to know how well this course or programme is suiting your needs. Please help us by giving brief answers to the questions below. If you want to say more, please use the back of the sheet. Thank you very much.

1. Which factors are helping you meet your goals?

2. What are you enjoying about your course/programme?

3. Which aspects have caused you difficulties?

4. How could the course or programme be improved for you?

5. Do you have any other comments which you'd like to make?

Preparing the students for evaluation

Students may need briefing in order to do justice to evaluation. They may not have had much experience of giving their views in this formal manner, and may be unsure how to phrase their comments. Forms should not be a test of language skills; use a rating scale if you think open questions will unfairly pressure your group. You may also need to remind students of the main learning activities, otherwise they may only remember the most recent ones. If you have been carrying out semi-formal monitoring activities with them over the year, you will have boosted their awareness of the evaluation process and their confidence in their ability to respond appropriately.

A huge bonus of evaluation is that the process itself can consolidate learning. It is often at this stage that learners see the point of what they have been doing. The process of structured reflection gives them an overview which they could not have attained at an earlier stage.

The longer view

Reassuring as assessment results are, and however interesting the immediate response to evaluation, the real test of your teaching and the students' learning is whether they can apply their learning in their working, studying or social lives. It can be quite difficult to discover this. You might think about a postal or telephone questionnaire after a reasonable period of time for application and reflection has passed.

The circular view

You will remember that we spoke of evaluation as **looking back in order to look forward**. Your evaluation findings will have put you more closely in touch with your students' learning needs. This in turn will lead you to reflect on your planning, to affirm or rethink the decisions you made originally. Next time round you may be making changes in how you implement those decisions. And so you go on around the cycle of teaching and training activities repeatedly.

Summary

You have now explored the purposes and processes of evaluation. By looking in detail at the evaluation of individual sessions and of complete programmes and courses of learning, you have learned to evaluate a large proportion of your own professional practice. Without the skills to review your own effectiveness, you are less empowered than your own students. Without the courage to act on your findings, you risk standing still in a rapidly developing profession.

11 Conclusions

You have now completed your journey round the stages of the teaching/training cycle. You will have noticed how one stage leads to the next, and have seen the links between particular stages, such as planning and assessment. You are now ready, with renewed energy and insight, to start again; for the end of the cycle is also its beginning.

You have had as companions on your journey a wide range of teachers and trainers keenly exploring approaches to their various work situations. You will have generated many ideas for your own teaching, as you shared in their problem solving and decision making. Perhaps you are now planning to put some of these ideas into operation?

Alternatively, you may now want to spend some time reflecting on what you have read, perhaps discussing certain issues with your students or your colleagues.

If you have found the ideas in this book stimulating, you may wish to take them further by investigating some of the texts in *Suggestions for Further Reading* at the end of the book. There is much more to explore about teaching and training, and even more about learning.

APPENDIX: Relationship between chapters and Training and Development NVQs/SVQs Levels 3 and 4

In the layout below, the relevant unit and element reference codes and titles are given in relation to each chapter. Heavy type indicates that this is the main material in the chapter; references in lighter type are to subsidiary material.

2 Getting Started

A22 Identify individual learning needs
>   **A221**   Identify available learning opportunities
>   **A222**   Identify learning needs with individuals

C21 Create a climate conducive to learning
>   **C211**   Establish rapport with learners
>   **C212**   Support learners' needs
>   **C213**   Promote access to learning and achievement
>   **C214**   Promote anti–discriminatory practice

A21 Identify individuals' learning aims, needs and styles
>   A211   Collect information from individuals on their learning aims, needs and styles
>   A212   Identify and agree individuals' learning aims, needs and styles

C26 Support and advise individual learners
>   C261   Provide guidance to help learners plan their learning
>   C263   Advise and support individual learners in managing their own learning

E41 Develop training and development methods
>   E411   Research ways in which people learn

3 Planning for Learning

This chapter contains brief guidance on all stages of the learning cycle so includes material which might be useful for units A21, A22, B31, C23–C27, D11, D21, D31–D33, E21, E23 and E31 as well as the detailed material below.

B21 Design learning programmes to meet learners' requirements
    B211   Select options for meeting learning requirements
    B212   Design learning programmes for learners
B22 Design training and development sessions
    B221   Identify options for training and development sessions
    B222   Design training and development sessions for learners
C11 Coordinate the provision of learning opportunities with other contributors to the learning programme
    C111   Agree roles and resources with contributors
    C112   Coordinate the activities of contributors

4   Teaching Aids and Learning Resources

B33 Prepare and develop resources to support learning
    B331   Prepare materials and facilities to support learning
    B332   Develop materials to support learning
B31 Design, test and modify training and development materials
    B312   Design training and development material
B211 Select options for meeting learning requirements
C231 Give presentations to groups

5   Presenting Information and Ideas

C23 Facilitate learning in groups through presentations and activities
    C231   Give presentations to groups
B332 Develop materials to support learning
C21 Create a climate conducive to learning
    C211   Establish rapport with learners
    C214   Promote anti-discriminatory practice
E23 Evaluate training and development sessions
    E231   Collect and analyse information on training and development sessions
E31 Evaluate and develop own practice
    E311   Evaluate own practice
E41 Develop training and development methods
    E412   Develop training and development methods to support different learning styles

6   Organising Learning in Groups

C23 Facilitate learning in groups through presentations and activities
    C232   Facilitate exercises and activities to promote learning in groups
C27 Facilitate group learning
    C271   Manage group dynamics
    C272   Facilitate collaborative learning
B33 Prepare and develop resources to support learning
    B331   Prepare materials and facilities to support learning

     B332   Develop materials to support learning
C211 Establish rapport with learners
C214 Promote anti-discriminatory practice
E231 Collect and analyse information on training and development sessions
E311 Evaluate own practice
E412 Develop training and development methods to support different styles of learning

7 Teaching a Skill

C24   Facilitate learning through demonstration and instruction
     C241   Demonstrate skills and methods to learners
     C242   Instruct learners
C25   Facilitate individual learning through coaching
     C251   Coach individual learners
     C252   Assist individual learners to apply their learning
C231 Give presentations to groups
C232 Facilitate exercises and activities to promote learning in groups
C211 Establish rapport with learners
C214 Promote anti-discriminatory practice

8 Supporting the Individual Learner

C22   Agree learning programmes with learners
     C221   Negotiate learning programmes with learners
     C222   Review learning programmes and agree modifications with learners
D11   Monitor and review progress with learners
     D111   Collect information on learners' progress
     D112   Conduct formative assessment with learners
     D113   Review progress with learners
C211 Establish rapport with learners
C212 Support learners' needs
C213 Promote access to learning and achievement
C26   Support and advise individual learners
     C261   Provide guidance to help individual learners plan their learning
     C262   Agree the roles and resources required to support the achievement of individual learning objectives
     C263   Advise and support individual learners in managing their own learning
A222 Identify learning needs with individuals
D211 Conduct non competence based assessment
D32   Assess candidate performance
D33   Assess candidate using differing sources of evidence

9   Assessing Achievement

D21   Conduct non competence based assessments
   D211   Conduct non competence based assessments
   D212   Analyse evidence to form assessment decision
   D213   Provide feedback to individuals on the assessment decision
D31   Design assessment methods to collect evidence of competent performance
   D311   Design assessment methods for the collection of performance evidence
   D312   Design assessment methods for the collection of knowledge evidence
D32   Assess candidate performance
   D321   Agree and review a plan for assessing performance
   D322   Collect and judge performance evidence against criteria
   D323   Collect and judge knowledge evidence
   D324   Make assessment decision and provide feedback
D33   Assess candidate using differing sources of evidence
   D331   Agree and review assessment plan
   D332   Judge evidence and provide feedback
   D333   Make assessment decision using differing sources of evidence and provide feedback
C213 Promote access to learning and achievement

10   Evaluation

E21   Evaluate training and development programmes
   E211   Select methods for evaluating training and development programmes
   E212   Collect information to evaluate training and development programmes
   E213   Analyse information to improve training and development programmes
E23   Evaluate training and development sessions
   E231   Collect and analyse information on training and development sessions
   E232   Improve training and development sessions
E31   Evaluate and develop own practice
   E311   Evaluate own practice
   E312   Identify self development needs
   E313   Adapt own practice to meet changes in training and development
D11   Monitor and review progress with learners
   D111   Collect information on learners' progress
   D112   Conduct formative assessment with learners
   D113   Review progress with learners
   C222   Review learning programmes and agree modifications with learners

Suggestions for Further Reading

General texts

MINTON, David. *Teaching Skills in Further and Adult Education*, Macmillan, London, 1991
(reprinted Thomson Learning 2000)
ROGERS, Jenny. *Adults Learning*, Open University Press, Milton Keynes, 3rd edition, 1989
SOTTO, Eric. *When Teaching Becomes Learning*, Cassell, London, 1994

Specialist texts

The education of adults

BROOKFIELD, Stephen, D. *Understanding and Facilitating Adult Learning*, Open University Press, Milton Keynes, 1986
JARVIS, Peter. *Adult and Continuing Education: Theory and Practice*, Croom Helm, London, 1983
SUTCLIFFE, Jeannie. *Adults with Learning Difficulties: Education for Choice and Empowerment*, NIACE, Leicester, 1991

Teaching and learning strategies

BOURNER, Tom, MARTIN, Vivien and RACE, Phil. *Workshops That Work*, McGraw-Hill, London, 1993
BROWN, George. *Lecturing and Explaining*, Methuen, London, 1983
FLEGG, David and McHALE, Josephine. *Selecting and Using Training Aids*, Kogan Page, London, 1991

Assessment

GIBBS, Graham, HABESHAW, Sue and HABESHAW, Trevor. *53 Interesting Ways To Assess Your Students*, Technical and Educational Services Ltd, Bristol, 1986
JESSUP, Gilbert. *Outcomes: NVQs and the Emerging Model of Education and Training*, The Falmer Press, London, 1991
WALKLIN, L. *The Assessment of Performance and Competence*, Stanley Thornes (Publishers) Ltd, Cheltenham, 1991

Index